HELMUT JAHN

HELMUT JAHN

Text by Nory Miller

RIZZOLI
NEW YORK

First published in the United States of America in 1986 by
RIZZOLI INTERNATIONAL PUBLICATIONS, INC.
597 Fifth Avenue, New York, NY 10017

Library of Congress Cataloging in Publication Data

Miller, Nory, 1947–
    Helmut Jahn.

    Bibliography: p.
    1. Jahn, Helmut, 1940–   2. Murphy/Jahn (Firm)
3. Architecture, Modern—20th century—United States.
I. Title.
NA737.J34M55   1986   720'.92'4   84-42787
ISBN 0-8478-0561-1
ISBN 0-8478-0562-X (pbk.)

Design by Keith Palmer
Composition by Roberts/Churcher, New York
Printed and bound in Japan

CONTENTS

INTRODUCTION

Wunderkinder inevitably generate curiosity. People want an explanation. What is the nature of this talent? How carefully orchestrated has been his climb? What can be handed off to luck? What to ability? What to ambition? Success in the young—especially enormous, visible, material success—whets appetites along with interest. Why him? underlies every other question.

Helmut Jahn has, not unwittingly, intensified this natural curiosity by developing for himself a flamboyant presence, both indicative and misleading as to his character. He runs in marathons, skis in Aspen, scuba dives off Australia's Great Barrier Reef and drives his Porsche fast enough to be in occasional jeopardy from the law. He wears his dark blond hair long enough to swashbuckle while encasing a lean and angular frame in gracefully cut Italian suits and the latest in foot and neckwear, assembled with an interior designer's eye for color and pattern. To this is added the small leather bag in which European gentlemen, but rarely Americans, keep their personal effects. Inside the bag, whatever the occasion, is a small sketchpad and a fat Mont Blanc fountain pen filled with brown ink. This latter characteristic is so frequently imitated by the young men who work for him that Jahn is moved to joke: "They all sign an agreement when they're hired that their first paycheck goes to buy the pen." Apparently the agreement extends to the untypical color of the ink, to judge by the evidence, and, occasionally, even leather bags and the architect's stiff, distinctive gait. Yet while this eager imitation attests to persuasiveness, the superstar imagery is perhaps decep-

tive. What has propelled Jahn from not particularly auspicious beginnings to his current power and prominence as an internationally-sought architect and head of a large, successful firm seems to have had as much to do with grueling hours, a facility for designing quickly and in series, and a gift for adapting to each situation as it arises, as it has with his taste for investing designs with the invention and rakish energy for which he has become famous.

Jahn was born in Nuremberg on January 4, 1940. The family lived in Allersberg, a farmer's village just outside. It was wartime and William Anton Jahn was a soldier. But after the fighting and a year as a prisoner of war in Philadelphia, he returned to his profession as a teacher of primary schoolchildren. The family, which now included two sons, moved to nearby Zirndorf. Helmut, the eldest, was rather a scamp, not above stealing materials from construction sites for youthful projects nor getting by in school on as little work as possible. Describing himself as neither a leader nor much of a reader, he remembers first considering a future in architecture at the gymnasium in Füth. There were three professions that interested him. Teaching was championed by his parents for the security it offered as state employment. His ambition to be an airline pilot seemed doomed by his lack of aptitude for languages. But an acknowledged facility for drawing suggested architecture. Having grown up at a time when his country was virtually a construction site as it struggled to rebuild and restore itself throughout most of his childhood, the choice must have seemed both practical and essen-

tial. But it was scarcely greeted with enthusiasm. The first teacher he mentioned it to laughed in response: "You'll never be an architect. You're too lazy. You should be a diplomat." The object lesson was provided apparently in the early weeks of architecture school. The first problem assigned was the design of a car porch. As Jahn tells it, he was just in the process of moving so he did a last minute tent with a handkerchief dyed tan supported on straws. Unexpectedly, the professor, not just his assistant, came to critique the projects and viewed the tent as an outrage and an insult, flattening it with his hand in disgust and not entirely amused when it popped back up. For the next problem, the chastened student drew a full set of pencil drawings of sufficient professional stature to earn Herr Professor's approbation. Both attitudes were to remain with him, both the tendency and ability to improvise designs quickly and the stamina to work almost constantly and expect little else from associates.

The path that led him to Chicago began with the reputation of the German emigre Ludwig Mies van der Rohe, whose pre-war distinction in Germany had now been supplemented with sizeable building projects in Chicago and New York and who was again working in his native country on the New National Gallery in Berlin. Jahn, by his own account, did not arrive in school a sophisticated student of architectural style or theory. The Munich Technische Hochschule, where he attended, emphasized the practical—programming, code problems, detailed drawings, thoroughness. Its professors ranged in sympathy along the full spectrum of design philosophy. But Jahn fell under the influence of a professor who enjoined him to emulate the work of Mies, sending him to the library to study details. After graduating in 1965, he went to work for an equally avid Munich architect, P. C. von Seidlein, for slightly longer than one year. There he met Dirk Lohan, Mies' grandson, and Birgitta Peterhans, who was married to the late Walter Peterhans, one of Mies' righthand men at the Illinois Institute of Technology (IIT). Their talk of Chicago and IIT, where Mies installed his architecture program, encouraged Jahn to see for himself. He won a one-year scholarship from the Rotary Club and was sent to school at IIT. In return, he travelled each week to a club meeting in the greater metropolitan area and gave a talk.

After half a year, and with a deadline for returning home, he was anxious to start his thesis. But such a time schedule was forbidden to those educated outside the institution's walls. He was advised to look for part-time work to keep himself busy instead. The job he found was answering the phones for Eugene Summers, a talented designer who had left Mies' office shortly before to open his own. But in January, 1967, C. F. Murphy Associates dangled the commission of the year in front of him and Summers closed up shop to join the busy and established firm. He took Jahn with him, not to answer phones but to work on McCormick Place II, a convention center for the city along Lake Michigan.

Jahn's early years at C. F. Murphy were as Summers' protege. There were other designers but by the time Summers left in 1973, few with responsibility on major projects had stayed. Before the year was out, Jahn had been named director of planning and design and his chief rival had accepted a job offer in Tulsa. The firm was in serious economic trouble, laying off staff and scrambling for work. Over the next decade, Jahn was instrumental in guiding the firm's transition from City Hall's palace architects, a role that had long been remunerative but—with the changes in Chicago politics—was no longer available, into a firm attractive to speculative developers and international design scouts.

The architects trained at IIT, not only by Mies but by his more doctrinaire colleagues, had been encouraged to think in terms of right and wrong. Clients had simply to be convinced or despaired of. But speculative commissions put a premium on adaptability—starting over from completely different premises every time a parcel of land was secured or not secured, a large tenant found or lost, a zoning decision made or challenged. A former partner describes the difference between Summers and his protege: "Gene would dig in his heels and be firm but Helmut just went back to the drawing board saying, 'There's more than one way to skin a cat.'" The difference between the two men, evident already in meetings on McCormick Place, partially reflects the difference between two generations—one trained by the masters of Modern architecture, the other in the liberating, if also confused, atmosphere following their deaths. Yet the difference is one of character as well. Jahn mellows his single-mindedness with a strong distaste for confrontation, for an approach that is intent but, in the long run, flexible.

From the beginning, it was clear that the stylistic direction of the firm, which Summers had expended great effort in effecting, was to be subject to a different set of values and interests. The younger man's first attributed building, the R. Crosby Sr. Memorial Arena in Kansas City, already indicated his ambivalence towards the work of Mies van der Rohe. Mies' Crown Hall at IIT, with its lightweight skin slung from a series of overarching girders is the source of Kemper's organization and structure. Yet Jahn takes the opportunity to exaggerate the tension between the frame and the box—an open network versus closed, solid pieces versus smooth skin, squared corners versus curved. If Mies enlisted industrial age materials in his pursuit of abstraction and inherent order, Jahn is genuinely drawn to machinery, the imagery and energy of mechanical devices. Mies' logic and clarity is reinterpreted in terms of muscular sensuality; his exacting elegance traded in for powerful expression.*

*The troublesome history of the building is well known but its resolution perhaps less so. In June 1979, more than one-third of its roof collapsed during a powerful storm but in the middle of the night such that, fortunately, no one was hurt. Ironically, the American Institute of Architects, a body that had previously conferred a national honor award on the building, was holding its convention in Kansas City at the time. After years of expert testimony at cross purposes, the financial questions were settled out of court without an official verdict as to the cause of the collapse. The arena has since been rebuilt by the arena's management with strengthened connections at what the management hopes are key points.

Similarly the truss wall of Jahn's Bartle Exhibition Hall in Kansas City, completed two years later, is adapted from Mies' 1953 convention hall project for Chicago. Yet the precise organization of Mies' unbuilt project is freely modified for irregular site conditions and contrast between materials and levels rather than integral continuity characterizes the execution.

Mies' loft buildings continued to be the major source for Jahn's work but the interpretation was increasingly irregular, dramatic and experimental. As in Mies' buildings, the Auraria and Michigan City libraries are generated a priori under the assumption that current and future building programs can be made to work within an unencumbered plan. But Auraria's elevations forego consistency to let windows, sunshades and louvers fall where they may in response to the angle of the sun and the light requirements of spaces within. And Michigan City's roofline is broken by a series of saw-toothed skylights—a move that distributes natural light throughout the library. The drama of the altered silhouette is intensified by arranging the skylights on a grid that runs at a diagonal to the grid of the building and then continuing the opposition on the interior with trusses, columns and fluorescent bulbs. The insulated but translucent plastic panels that mask the library's undistinguished surroundings were used again at St. Mary's Athletic Center. But these were to be the last of Jahn's projects where the material appears for, despite his enthusiasm for new materials and processes, the panels proved less than impervious to scratching.

Color has been another area of experiment. Mies' palette of neutrals was abandoned in favor of the bright new world coming over from England and Europe. The electric shades of Norman Foster and his various colleagues had already influenced such American firms as the iconoclastic Hardy, Holzman and Pfeiffer. But Jahn undertook the experiment one step at a time. First, color appeared in the interior, on oversized airducts and pipes in crayola technicolor. Then it gingerly emerged on the exterior: the courts building in Maywood was anodized a deep plum; the red columns and roof structure on the interior of St. Mary's is offset just enough to show through the glass from outside. Finally, the stops were pulled out completely and De La Garza blazed dayglo in the midst of one of the country's most depressed inner cities. Chromatic understatement was never to hold an allure for Jahn again. The few exceptions in the built work represent client vetoes. Xerox, for instance, was designed as a blue tower and the flat black columns of One South Wacker were bright red in the architect's model.

Honesty of materials had become another of Mies' absolutes that no longer was held inviolable. Despite the fact that the garage and office buildings for Commonwealth Edison were constructed of different materials, they were arranged and colored to seem interchangeable and uniform.

Yet despite the highly visible digressions from Mies' precedent, structure continued to be emphatic; plans continued to be gridded, and detailing the skin of each building continued to be a central concern. What was beginning to change was the primacy of shape—not just the particular shape that Mies favored, the rectangle—but preconceived, perceivable shape in any sense. Both Maywood and De La Garza are based on a bolt of cloth approach, in which future expansion is assumed and expressed in end walls that differ markedly from the presumably permanent front and back. It was a decided departure from Mies whose suggested infinite rearrangements of the interior were predicated on carefully chosen shapes and consistent elevations. It looked instead beyond the image of the factory to its open-ended, utilitarian modus operandi and, along with that, to its erector set rawness—interests that were far more prevalent in England and his native Germany than in Jahn's adopted country at the time.

If shape, however, was to be downplayed as an organizing principle, another needed to be found. From the mid- to late-1970s, circulation was to fill that role in Jahn's work. It was a logical outcome of an architecture viewed not as an object but as an arbitrary moment in a changing (read growing) situation. If the advocates of mega-structures were the most eloquent spokesmen for this point of view, Candilis, Josic, Woods' Free University in Berlin was possibly the most practical demonstration. For Jahn the rationale was in a sense fortuitous. Beginning with his headquarters for Rustoleum, circulation spines became the most prominent elements in his mat (low) buildings, with volumes hinged onto them in various configurations. That this organization was not primarily dictated by an urgent need to provide for expansion is suggested by the happenstance that none of these buildings has since been enlarged. Even in a finite setting, however, the protuberant circulation spines charged essentially static shapes with directional energy and, within the buildings, placed movement back and forth on center stage. The potential for this kind of animation held such appeal for Jahn that he experimented with the linearity of both protruding corridors and rows of skylights for several years, sometimes within and sometimes without the context of buildings with discernible overall shapes. It was only later, through the intermediary of historicism, that Jahn rediscovered his interest in the potential for buildings considered as designed objects.

In his next building and in several after that, Jahn's assimilative approach to design became ever clearer. Fascinated with architecture, but dedicated to no single theoretical stance, he partook eagerly of the various proposals percolating in the divided and mutable architectural circles around him. Permeable to both the practical and the exalted, Jahn transmogrifies each with his own taste for tangibility, contrast and even a certain impudence. When the aftermath of the 1974 oil embargo plunged architects into an era of thermal responsibility, Jahn's response was immediate and enthusiastic but more willful than evangelistic. Never tempted by the anti-modern, anti-urban wing of the profession's energy lobby, he nonetheless happily involved himself in using sunlight to illuminate his buildings and installing increasingly efficient mechanical systems. That the ragged angles of skylights could mean a more interesting profile or that atria

might offer interior drama or at least relief were aesthetic possibilities hardly lost on him. The utilitarian advantages of technology remained stepping stones to expressions of its excitement. And excitement, to Jahn, meant clashing formal relationships. When he opened the roof of Michigan City's library, he closed the sides, and then set each on irreconcilable geometric journeys. At Argonne, the skylights, rather than being integrated into the whole composition, are made to erupt rudely out of a roof that has not seemingly anticipated the development. Even on the proposed United Air Lines Terminal at O'Hare, angles are set against curves and horizontal glazing against vertical. Atria are similarly picked out and employed for maximum impact: canted and copper-toned at One South Wacker; enormous, uncloaked and through the roof at the State of Illinois Center.

There is an impish, tongue-in-cheek quality to his versions of the far more dicey assignment to invest architecture with symbolism. To the unproselytizing Jahn, who undertakes the perceived obligation of rhetoric with a certain misgiving, this was not interpreted as an opportunity to communicate points of view. Rather he translated the call for meaning in architecture as a call for recognizable images. There are designs where one might suspect that any discussion of image was after the fact, such as the "sun" plan of Argonne, a shape dictated less poetically by a desire to minimize the perimeter to volume ratio of a building intended as an exemplar of energy conservation. But there are others, such as the U. S. Post Office in Oak Brook or the Area II police station,

which are presented almost entirely in terms of imagery. Jahn's first design for the addition to the Board of Trade, where enormous fortunes are made and lost, rather resembled a cash register; and a speculative office building for a real estate arm of the De Beers' conglomerate in Johannesburg is purposely rendered in the form of a diamond. What architectural symbolism offered to Helmut Jahn was never so much a means to convert or even remind but a method of making choices—choices of color or shape or pattern—from among the endless possibilities.

"There's a square, a triangle and a circle. That's all God gave us," is a frequent pronouncement of the architect as he hovers over a drawing board just as "Isn't there anything else?" is the phrase that accompanies searches through the office, combing through drawings and models of previous designs for hints to help shape a current one. Unlike many architects, Jahn generally designs in series. He submitted not one but six designs to the Bank of the Southwest Tower Competition; three different towers for Frankfurt Messe, and four for Philadelphia. Each series is a virtual study in geometrical manipulation, begun generally with elements from previous designs that are then combined, recombined, nipped and tucked until the designer and clients are satisfied.

The pattern of repetition and restlessness began long before Jahn worked on the building type for which he has become most famous—the speculative tower. But it is a pattern uncannily suited to the type and the architect fully realizes it. "You have to accept the fact," he offers, "that when people hire you to do new and different things, you can't go around defending one kind of thing and develop a philosophy around it. If I had a philosophy, all the buildings would be the same. The only way to succeed in this area is to satisfy people who want something fresh and flamboyant for marketing. The programmatic requirement is to do something that stands apart, an anti-thing."

Underlying the range of imaginative design is Jahn's persistent systematization. Whether a result of the categorization that is taught in German schools in every subject and at every level, or a methodology of his own, it is the filter through which he looks at buildings. Jahn's early work can be seen as an exploration of potential modifications to Mies' box—an exploration encompassing curved, punctured, eroded and folded surfaces in various amalgamations. But it was only a prelude to the geometric manifestations that were to follow. Yet, as always with Jahn, the evolution began tentatively and proceeded step by step.

Xerox Centre, designed in 1978 and Jahn's first highrise, is relatively straightforward. Faced with a corner site and a profession increasingly adamant about fitting buildings into their physical contexts, Jahn reorganized the more typical slab tower as a quarter circle. Turning the corner with a curve, a choice with ample pedigree from Beaux Arts to Eric Mendelsohn, remains one of his two responses to such sites, though the simple curve has undergone considerable elaboration. (The alternate response is an octagon, facing the corner with one of the elevations.)

The curve at Xerox is made more emphatic by the detailing of the elevation that provides taller windows around the corner and much of the north face, a response to climate and interior views as well as form. In addition, the shaft has been kinked slightly, adjustments suggested by parking needs as well as a desire to relate to the rooflines of adjacent buildings. This strategy is similar, on the one hand, to Kevin Roche's United Nations Plaza, completed three years earlier, in which the tower is regarded as a jigsaw puzzle piece to be fitted into the city. At the same time, it reflects the ambivalence toward an *a priori* shape seen in the architect's mat buildings of the period.

For the quite different task of uniting the hotel and office building at First Bank Center in South Bend, Jahn enlisted and adapted elements from his contemporaries: the atrium webbing stretched between the twin towers of Johnson/Burgee's Pennzoil Place in Houston; and the exposed glass hotel elevators made famous by Atlanta's John Portman. However, it was the thrill of the ride provided by the elevators that attracted Jahn, not their jewelry-like execution, and his versions are considerably more stolid.

Later that year, the commission to design an addition to Chicago's Board of Trade encouraged Jahn for virtually the first time to pay close attention to historical design, which was to become an important aspect of his work. He had flirted with merging Georgian allusions and shiny modernity for the University of Illinois building, but his client proved less context than cost-conscious, and the design was con-

siderably watered down. The Board, on the other hand, insisted that any new building relate to its landmark art déco tower in detail. Jahn's first design took characteristic ornament from the tower's lobby and blew it up to building size. The design was rejected out of hand by the client, although it was to appear and reappear in the schematic stages of subsequent buildings and in the details of this one. The final design emulated not only the elder building's ornament but its organization, rhythms, materials and pinnacle.

Its irony is that as much as it resembles the stately landmark, it resembles it hardly at all. The new building's elevations include some stone screenwall but mostly it is mirror glass standing in for the limestone of the 1930 tower; gypsum board with trim on the interior standing in for marble and metal ornament; and off-the-shelf light fixtures dictating Rubenesque proportions where El Greco's would have been more in keeping. As in many contemporary historicist designs, attitude and training as well as budget made it necessary to approach history in a classics comics version—simplified, *sans gravitas,* and translated into common parlance.

Afterwards, Jahn continued to delve into history for architectural inspiration though he went back and forth between historicist and modern design even as he went back and forth between periods of history. Each period, however, provided him with increasingly complex geometries to integrate. Louis Sullivan's broad reverberating entry arches are the source for Northwestern's grand portal. Adolf Loos' submission to the Chicago Tribune Competition of 1922 suggested the profile for 425 Lexington Avenue and Egyptian obelisks the profile of Park Avenue Tower. The domed capitol buildings of Washington, D.C. and many state capitals led Jahn to his design for the State of Illinois Center. And photographs of London's 1879 Burlington Arcade shaped the retail floors at the office tower in Durban, South Africa. More generally, the symmetry, hierarchy and grand scale of the Beaux Arts became the stepping off point for a number of designs even as the search lights from Hugh Ferriss' utopian visions appeared in the background of Jahn's presentation drawings.

At no time did Jahn become an advocate of traditional design as preferable to modern design. To him, historical architecture presented not a choice but choices—choices that were essentially geometrical, material and organizational rather than sentimental and whole. While his American, English and South African colleagues might turn to traditional architecture as a preference, a reminder of worlds they were part of or would like to have been, Jahn turned to nothing from the past that could have had any personal significance. His own youth had been spent in Germany at a time when its bombed out cities were being rebuilt in a kind of debased Swedish modern. But neither that nor ruins nor traditional German architecture appear in his work.

What does appear is from other people's pasts: their childhood in Chicago amidst its immense stone structures; their prix-de-Rome year in Italy; their defiant nostalgia for the scorned exuberances of art déco. Jahn's assimilative approach has accepted each though he readily admits that "the historical and futurist buildings are actually the same. The Board of Trade is a Mies box transformed to fit." And the Greyhound Bus Terminal is actually Kemper in Kew Gardens drag. They are the same, first of all, because the underlying construction techniques and modular organization is the same. But they are also the same because, by being someone else's past, the visions are no more full-bodied than an imagined future.

Whereas Mies abstracted images that were real to him, images of neo-classical architecture lining the streets and academies of his own youth, Jahn genuinely thinks in terms of abstract geometry: minimal sculpture geometry, art déco revival geometry, Beaux Arts geometry. The difference between abstracting from what is real and arranging abstractions to approximate it is never more apparent than when he undertakes the difficult task of rethreading representation back into architecture. As there is no particular effect that Jahn is attempting to reproduce, he dissects, merges and abstracts until resemblance can no longer be misunderstood as the point.

In contrast, in his blatantly "futurist" buildings—whether inspired by constructivist work from early in the century or Norman Foster's from last year—Jahn emerges as a genuinely lyrical designer. While he is specific and believable as to his lack of "missionary feeling that this or that is the building of the future," he is clearly exhilarated by the look, surge, and intricate toughness of machinery. His taste in technology celebrates its energy not its ability to line up and count off; its headstrong defiance not its logic. In Jahn's hands, technology is more spirited than fun; decorative only on its way to being animated, and never so docile as to be mistaken for utilitarian.

In his practice, however, the approaches to design are equally valued. Generally the choice has something to do with the project's site. The Frankfurt Hyatt-Regency, therefore, reflects the cornice heights, fenestration and stone of the landmark office buildings with which it shares the block while Jahn's design for a convention center on San Diego's waterfront bristles with masts and cables, portholes and primary color. Other times, the choice is determined by competition strategies, a challenge Jahn admits enjoying almost more than design. His Humana entry, for instance, took Tatlin's Monument to the Third International project into the corporate world as an alternative to fellow contestant Michael Graves who "was sure to go historical." After Graves did "go historical" and did win, the model was spotted by the client who had commissioned the office building in Johannesburg. A modified version, with gardens at every level and a concrete structural system, became 326 West Street in Durban.

Durban (and Humana) were also the product of another quest that has been fundamental in shaping Jahn's towers: the struggle to render undeniably huge buildings congenial. Designing skyscrapers in the latter quarter of the twentieth century is to design in the face of the criticism and disillusionment that lately has accompanied the products of the century's earlier starry-eyed enthusiasm. The broad censure of highrises as being sterile, alienating and overpowering has put architects in something of a quandary, trying to remove the sting from size when size itself is non-negotiable. One approach calls for designing buildings that blend into the background, but Jahn is neither temperamentally suited to erecting diffident and unassuming design nor perhaps gullible about its attainability. Instead he has largely taken the approach of dissecting each volume into discernible and smaller pieces that, only in their interaction, amass as a single structure. The geometric routes this subterfuge can take are open-ended and Jahn has investigated first one, then another and so on in series.

One South Wacker represents a transition between Xerox's rough-edged homogeneity and the course the later towers were to take. It is of-a-piece yet folded back and crowned to suggest something more like a triptych. The setbacks and emphatic atria (used here not out of necessity as at the earlier Board of Trade Addition, but as a marketing device) further section the silhouette, though the variations in glass color and reflectivity are almost too subtle to read. The Northwestern Tower is a more compelling refinement of the triptych and setback technique, but its skin was redesigned sufficiently over the years that construction was delayed by a protest over the supposed landmark quality of the railroad building marked for demolition, that this aspect is best discussed later.

The Johannesburg "diamond" is an outgrowth of One South Wacker in the sense that a single form has been cut and shaped to offer modulations of dimension and rhythm. But closely following Johnson/Burgee's Garden Grove Community Church (better known as the Crystal Cathedral), 11 Diagonal Street's gestures are stronger, symmetrical and, in short, crystalline. The design began entirely as a geometric investigation; only when a diamond-like form began to emerge did Jahn consider the connection.

With 701 Fourth Street in Minneapolis, Jahn literally unhinges elements of the tower, wrapping one around the other and visually taping them together with mullions and spandrels. Additionally, he superimposes a larger than life grid on the outer layer (a la Arquitectonica's Atlantis in Miami) to create the optical illusion of a much smaller building. The wrapping of one form around another is used again in versions of Americana Plaza and adapted for Shand Morahan. Then, in schematics for his Bank of the Southwest Tower entry, Jahn pursues the concept further, emphasizing either the fixed tension of two interlocked elements or the spiral thrust of a building wrapping around itself. The winner among Jahn's six entries was from the former series, itself an inverse version of the emblematic Empire State Building in which the corners retreat and the inner shaft declares victory from the ground up. The spiral series developed first into Humana and then Durban.

The winning Southwest entry is also characterized by a second level of disassociation—base from shaft from capital—to a degree only hinted at in earlier work. The applicability of these disjunc-tions to the sky exposure plane zoning of midtown Manhattan yielded the solid bases and slimmer towers of 425 Lexington and Park Avenue. Though quite different in profile—one is based on the archetype of the column, the other on the obelisk—their organizations are quite similar. Each is divided vertically and horizontally into three sections. And each pushes the contrast between corners and faces until they seem to belong to entirely different buildings that have somehow become tangled up in each other.

The tangling of supposedly unrelated structures is investigated not only in terms of the detailing of the skin, but also in terms of the shaping of the volumes in the designs of both Wilshire/Midvale and Unifirst Center. In these projects various buildings seem to have drifted into each other and merged.

The latest projects continue to refine these techniques for investing immense structures with calibrated proportions. Each of the three towers submitted for the Frankfurt Messe competition surround an inner glass core with an outer wrapping. Two of the wrappings combine stone and glass. The third is a superstructure with some of the same optical ambitions as the supergrids in Minneapolis and Durban. Similarly, two of the Philadelphia schemes present inner cores surrounded by outer layers, a third combines the wrapped core idea with a columnar profile, and the fourth—setting corner against plane—looks to Mayan pyramids to tame the monolith.

Interestingly, at the same time as the architect was searching for ways to make big buildings seem smaller, he was often subconsciously designing low buildings as if they were skyscrapers. The most obvious example is Shand Morahan, a cut-down version of several unbuilt highrise projects. But his handsome house for then-partner Robert Murphy is less obviously but unmistakably a skyscraper in miniature. Its elevations consist of regular frames into which windows or panels or lattice are inserted as infill. The interior is essentially modular loft space with a central core—the stairs. Indeed, the dimension of the cube is 30 feet—also the typical bay width of office towers.

At the same time, Jahn continued to look to his earlier mat buildings for guidance in designing more recent ones. Parktown Stands coalesces an early scheme for the Oak Brook Post Office with the skin from his Codex Corporation competition entry, the skylights from Argonne and an earthy color scheme inspired by the surrounding landscape. The blend created a pair of quite striking, lively and well-proportioned suburban office buildings.

As Jahn has watched his projects turn into buildings, however, he has faced and developed criticisms of his own. Just as the weathering deficiencies of the insulated plastic panels at Michigan City led him to choose glass block for the Area II police station and to investigate still other materials for the proposed United Terminal at O'Hare, the translation of his earliest towers from seductive models to full-scale reality have led to questions about certain aspects of their design. The flush mirror skins, though fashionable in the profession both at the time and since, proved to have the unfortunate byproduct of rein-

venting oil canning thirty years after it had been overcome. The mirror glass at both the Board of Trade Addition and One South Wacker had such a glittery effect that it undercut the buildings' substantiality and specific form. And distorted reflections of the straight lines of neighboring buildings turned out to be far less pleasant than the vague outlines of reflected clouds above. Moreover, the size and distribution of budget led to curtain wall detail which the firm has steadfastly avoided since. The elevations of the Board of Trade Addition, for instance, are detailed in stick-like snap-on mullions with a break in the middle of each unit filled with what the firm's architects refer to unsympathetically as "chewing gum"—a flexible compound to permit expansion and contraction.

Subsequent designs are virtual research projects in alternatives. By early 1982, when the first towers were well above ground, two other mullion types appeared on the drawing boards, often in combination with flat mullions or silicone glazing. Both are deeper and heftier than the snap-ons. One is a half-round, the other a full round. Though conceptually similar to Mies' famous I-beam mullions, Jahn became interested in the half-round after watching the rather successful skin of a new Chicago tower by Kohn Pederson & Fox, and in the full round from photographs of Norman Foster's recent project for Hong Kong.

Jahn's reliance on mirror glass has been tempered with a keener interest in less reflective materials. During the design of the Bank of the Southwest for which his client had specifically required a stone base, Jahn became knowledgeable and

interested in the potential of stone to enrich the texture and sturdy appearance of buildings at the street level where people come in closest contact with them. Though the architect had employed stone screen walls at the Board of Trade Addition, he had used them largely for their symbolic effect. With a client who was intensely interested in the sentiment and aesthetic of the material itself, Jahn looked at stone in a completely new way. Stone was a material that came in many different colors and each could be rough-cut, flamed or polished. It was three-dimensional and could be carved into shapes that projected or tapered. It could be incised. At Shand Morahan the architect used the three-dimensionality to solve a problem that had disturbed him at Xerox. The earlier tower had met the ground with a discrete reveal that was of necessity then filled with sealant. Shand Morahan meets the ground with a solid foot of granite on the theory that "if the bottom is strong, the goo won't detract." In addition, the technology of erecting stone in thin sheets on an aluminum curtainwall had reached the level where it was physically interchangeable with glass and no longer economically prohibitive.

While designing the office tower at Durban, Jahn discovered another material that has become part of the current repertoire: textured glass. Textured glass, like mirrored, has some of the opaqueness of stone while retaining the lightness and light-filled quality of clear glass. Yet it avoids the distortions and tinsel-like brittleness of mirror. When a budget crunch changed Northwestern's windows from a 2½-foot width to 5 feet—a dimension at which oil canning is completely out of control—its previously designed skin was scrubbed. The new one incorporates textured glass and full, round, popped-out mullions.

In the intervening years, elaborate skins have gone beyond the therapeutic to become exciting in themselves to the architects. Jahn finds the contrast of stone against glass "exaggerated and refreshing." The potential of incorporating changes of color (in mullions, glass and stone) along with textural changes has led to increasingly textile-like woven skins in plaid, checked and other patterns offering simultaneous messages at various scales.

At the same time, the firm is far more involved in both the approach and the interior even of speculative buildings. The entry to One South Wacker, for instance, is a larger version of the excavation from within the building envelope that Jahn used at Xerox. The semblance of an arcade is simply pasted on the sides as a scale device. In contrast, the Americana Plaza is provided with grand gateways; the State of Illinois Center has a surrealist forecourt of eroding granite piers; and Wilshire/Midvale has an artificially-lit solarium with a fountain in the middle to welcome pedestrians and an equivalently formal *porte cochere* for drivers.

The increasingly embellished lobbies may owe as much to the demands of the Southwest Bank, which kept sending designs back asking if they couldn't be a little richer, and to the return of designers specializing in interiors, as to Jahn's own predilections. But the dignified lobby design for Southwest, the festive two-story arcade for Durban and the firm's elegant new offices for itself are ample demonstration of the direction.

How Jahn will react when these new directions are realized as finished buildings awaits their completion. He views architecture much as scientists view research, a question of trial and error. "When Mies built glass buildings," he points out, "they were hothouses. There was no air-conditioning. The single panes froze up in winter and leaked." Moreover, he is acutely aware of the pitfalls of attempting traditional design with contemporary construction. "Without historical materials and craftsmanship," he says, "it's a high wire act. You're working without a net."

Meanwhile, Jahn's practice has expanded from Chicago to the Midwest, from the Midwest to the nation, and from the U.S. to Europe and South Africa. His felicitous hand, speed and instinct for high impact design recommend him to the developers and corporations he calls "the Medicis of this age." At the same time that zest for the new discourages the longer, slower process of refining each concept and each form until it has the irrefutable presence that work by masters such as Mies has. It is perhaps this that explains why Jahn has had an easier time convincing clients than colleagues, though Mies has scarcely escaped criticism from the architectural community through his efforts.

Helmut Jahn's future is one of the most difficult to predict. As an architect, he is genuinely open to formal exploration, innovative technique, new materials and rearranging priorities. He has shown that he can and will adjust his ideas as he gains experience from seeing his designs built. And, more than most architects, he is garnering experience at an extraordinary clip. Moreover, Jahn is only 45 years old, an age when many architects really begin their personal careers. What is clear is that he has already built an international practice; oversees every aspect of a firm in which he delegates effort but not decisions; and enjoys eminence in one of the era's most prominent and volatile specialties within architecture—a specialty for which his talents and temperament are particularly well-suited.

THE OFFICE

The office of Murphy/Jahn was not initiated by Helmut Jahn but fashioned out of a large, established and quite different firm, C. F. Murphy Associates. The strong opinions of Jahn's predecessor and mentor Eugene Summers and the aftershocks of a local and national recession that almost dismantled the firm in the early 1970s were significant influences, along with Jahn's own enthusiasms and predilections, on the evolution that began when he was still a junior staff member and continued under his direction patiently and ineluctably as he emerged first as head designer, then heir apparent and finally, only last year, as proprietor.

The firm Jahn became heir to had been inherited many times before. In a reasonably direct line, it dates back to no less than the great Daniel H. Burnham, Chicago's revered planner and legendary big business architect whose collaboration with designers John Wellborn Root and Charles Atwood gave the city some of its finest buildings. When Burnham died in 1912, his long-time associate Ernest Graham founded the successor firm Graham, Burnham and Company with the late architect's two sons. When they left in 1917, Graham re-formed the firm as Graham, Anderson, Probst and White with survivors of the original office.

Meanwhile, in 1911, Charles Murphy, an ambitious young man from one of the city's south side Irish neighborhoods had broadened his opportunities with stenographic training and a job in the Burnham typing pool. When Graham took over the firm a year later, Murphy became his private secretary and, in time, his right hand man. On the side he went to night school and acquired an architectural license.

Graham continued to direct the big, successful office, encouraging young men, especially Murphy, Sigurd Naess and Alfred Shaw, by giving them increasing responsibility. When he died in 1936, the name partners—furious for years at the favoritism—fired their rivals and changed the locks. They kept the name Graham, Anderson, Probst and White—a firm that continues today. The younger men rented space in the same building, formed Shaw, Naess & Murphy, and took over the biggest job in the office—a renovation of Atwood's Museum of Science and Industry. The hostility between the two firms was sufficiently intense that Murphy, who had been named executor of Graham's estate, had to threaten suit to gain entry to the records in Graham's filing cabinets. That estate funded The Graham Foundation for Advanced Studies in Art and Architecture, a foundation Murphy organized according to the provisions of the will and continued to oversee.

Two connections imbued the firm with national stature: a political connection to Chicago's long-term mayor Richard J. Daley that helped funnel the best civic commissions through its doors; and a design connection to several of the best products of Mies van der Rohe's school (the Illinois Institute of Technology) and office. When Daley first came to power he was looking for new faces to ally with. He was from the same neighborhood as Charles Murphy though young enough not to have been his schoolmate. The first commission Daley brought Naess and Murphy (Shaw had by then left to found his own shop) was a problem project—a filtration plant on the lakefront which citizen groups were contesting in court. When the firm's proposal—a landfill park setting for the plant (Stanislaw Gladych, designer)—resulted in neighborhood approval, Daley gained a confidence in the firm he was not to lose. Many commissions followed, including a new airport and government office towers, though the assignments were often split among several firms—a modification dictated by politics.

The firm first acquired its reputation as part of Mies' legacy when it hired his talented ex-student Jacques Brownson. His design for the Richard J. Daley Center (nee Civic Center) established both Brownson and the firm as worthy descendants. The hiring of Brownson, however, had not signified a change in ideological position. Other designers in the firm tended towards Brutalist work and even Edward Durell Stone-inspired exotica and the firm remained loyal to each.

Under Charles Murphy Sr., who renamed the firm after himself when Naess retired in 1959, the firm had developed into a mighty institution with subsidiary firms for civil engineering, construction management and, eventually, interiors. The mechanical, structural and electrical engineers and production departments were held in such high repute that the office received many commissions to back up other firms with engineering and/or working drawings. The firm's commissions were almost entirely local but they were numerous enough to support an office of as many as 450 people throughout much of the 1960s. These people were, as in most other firms at the time, organized into departments: design, architecture (working drawings), estimating, scheduling and so forth. Most of the top administrative and design people were permitted to buy small quantities of stock but it was understood that control of the firm was to be handed down to Murphy's sons: Charles Jr., who had an architectural degree from Notre Dame, and Robert.

It was another Mies-trained designer who began to change the organization. Brownson had left to take on experiments in prefabrication and economies of scale for the Board of Education, and later, the deanship at the University of Michigan. Other Mies-influenced designers had been hired, but none of Brownson's stature. Carter Manny, the IIT graduate who had introduced Brownson to the firm and who was rising within its ranks to the title of senior vice-president, tried to interest one of Mies' associates, Eugene Summers, in joining the opposition. Summers declined, left Mies and formed his own firm, hiring IIT student Helmut Jahn part-time to answer the phones. After months without sufficient work, Summers received a phone call from Murphy executive Hans Neumann. It was 1967. The city's convention hall, McCormick Place, had burnt down. Murphy had received the commission for the new building. Would Gene like to design it? This time the answer was yes.

The young part-timer came along to the firm and graduated from answering phones to assisting on the widely-acclaimed McCormick Place II. Summers did not like the firm's practice of backing up projects designed by other firms. Possible joint ventures on Sears Tower and Standard Oil were rejected. He favored an organization based on project teams. And, perhaps most important, he pushed the firm toward a uniform approach to design under his control.

Then in the early 1970s, the firm showed signs of collapsing. Several of the biggest jobs in the firm came to a natural end, and there was little to replace them. The oil embargo in 1973 and the recession that followed hit architectural firms hard and fast. By mid-1973 Murphy Associates was down to half-strength and falling. At its lowest point, it employed only 93 people. The now elderly Murphy Sr. was semi-retired. Summers saw an opportunity and tried to buy the firm but was rebuffed. He left to form Ridgeway Development Corporation with his long-time friend from Mies' office, Bronfman heiress Phyllis Lambert.

Jahn stayed, along with John Novak, a designer of roughly the same status. The firm's offices in other midwestern cities were closed. The civil engineering firm was sold to its top man. Four or five more lean years followed during which Jahn's position as head designer and major force in the firm was consolidated. Novak left to work for a former client.

Today the firm estimates its current construction volume at $300-$400 million with another $400 million on the drawing boards. But the streamlining forced on the firm during the crunch has become a way of life. The size has been gradually increased to 130 people, of whom 38 are now employed by the joint venture for the O'Hare airport expansion. The philosophy is to maintain a close line on staffing, to grow from within and to avoid layoffs.

The engineering departments have been phased out. This began actively in 1981, when the firm's name was officially changed, and Jahn was made President, but it had been allowed to proceed by attrition for years as the firm was no longer accepting back-up commissions. As a young architect, Jahn has found it easier to hire outside consultants than to wage personal and political contests with fellow employees often of much longer tenure. This approach has meshed well with the increasing workload from speculative developers who generally have an assortment of consultants firmly in mind.

The staff is organized into teams headed by project architects who combine the roles of project manager, designer and job captain. Each team is assigned to a building through completion but extra staff may be added to the nucleus during production. In general, the teams are kept small and work around the clock if necessary to avoid layers of supervision. In a profession given to overtime and high-pressure deadlines, Murphy/Jahn has earned a reputation for requiring more out of its staff than almost any other, an outgrowth perhaps of Jahn's own prodigious output. On the whole, the firm is a young office. While a third of the staff that survived the recession is still with the firm, many of the newer members arrived fresh out of school. No longer do they come exclusively from IIT, which supplied most of the firm's workforce during Summers' tenure, but from a variety of schools all over the country.

Jahn alone is responsible for conceptual design. With him at all times are a 4¼″ by 5½″ pad (one-quarter of a letter-size page) and a Mont Blanc pen filled with brown ink. He sketches, by his own description, on airplanes, in taxi cabs, at meals, in the office and out. The process often results not in one proposal but in a series of alternatives, each of which is then developed by the project team for presentation to the client. Generally there are between two and five alternatives but one is often refined further than the others and presented as the forerunner. The sketches Jahn hands to his staff describe plan, elevation, section, bay sizes, module, and often complex detailing for the skin or corner at a scale of inches. The involvement of the project architects in the design varies with the individual. Jahn's most trusted associate, James Goettsch, has been with the firm almost as long as Jahn and enjoys a unique position as a loyal devil's advocate.

Model building has been the traditional design tool of the office. Models vary from 1/50th to 1/8th with occasional full-size mock-ups of details. Model photographs are considered study tools as well as documentation. More recently, wall-size drawings—both perspectives and elevations—have been added to help designers visualize the final product. A project such as the Johannesburg speculative office building involved no fewer than 20 models. While younger team members construct cardboard models, presentation models are prepared by three full-time modelmakers and a student helper. There are three or four senior architects titled Managers of Production who work out de-

tails and overlook the production of working drawings. Director of Production and Quality is Samuel Scaccia, a member of the firm since 1963.

The shift in clientele underlies many of the organizational changes. The local political situation has, for the several years since Daley's death, been both volatile and underfunded. The firm has reached out for commissions beyond the Midwest, and, like many large firms in the past decade, to speculative developers of downtown towers. The nature of these projects—they have simple, repetitive programs, they require eye-catching marketable images; they are undertaken by entrepreneurs in a position to make instantaneous decisions in a business that is fast-moving and high risk—has helped determine the current organization of the firm. It has less need at the moment for people who would work diligently with the various echelons of a client organization to figure out what is needed and how the various functions interact. The staff is small and prepared to work overtime in order to react efficiently when projects are suddenly dead, revived, enlarged, shrunk and due yesterday. Of 20 designs, three may go ahead. Fewer production drawings are needed as many components are standard—a distinct change from a project such as the Civic Center, which was in Jahn's words "detailed down to the light switches." The single project leader can meet with the single entrepreneur to work out solutions that each can act upon immediately. In recent years, speculative office towers have been not only the most profitable form of architectural practice but the most readily available. Jahn's

position is that the firm fits its current clients and must be prepared to change for potentially different clients in the future.

Public and private competitions now play a large role in the firm's business as well. These have become more frequent, especially limited ones with invited entrants. As the European attitude towards competition as a prestigious impetus for the evolution of design has penetrated American practice, large firms that once shunned the not particularly profitable enterprise have embraced it enthusiastically. Moreover, the removal of the AIA injunction against wooing clients with sketches before being hired has opened the door to quasi-competitions between rivals for a particular job.

For Murphy/Jahn, formal and informal competitions have virtually replaced the brochure and other conventional business development methods. In the process, the advantage has shifted from firms with track records to firms whose designs are both distinctive and produced quickly. Jahn's proposition to potential clients is that every design, whatever the size or type of building, will essentially be by his hand.

Support functions continue to be organized by department but those departments have been both whittled and fused by the experience of the 1970s. Instead of a staff of 11 in accounting, there are four people and a computer and their responsibilities include personnel, office and financial management. The book library has been abandoned and the specifications department keeps track of samples. The audio-visual department has been reduced to one person, a veteran employee and licensed architect, who is in charge of promotion, business development, the print shop, messengers and photography. The print shop, consisting of two diazo machines, photocopy and offset presses, can be available at any hour.

Photography is a special support function because Jahn himself is interested in it and, in the early days, often photographed his own buildings for publication. Today, photographers are not hired by the day; James Steinkamp and Keith Palmer (who also heads Promotion and Business Development) are on staff. Jahn continues to offer a good deal of direction, often with drawings to show the angles from which shots should be taken.

The unique history of the interiors department has obtained the distinction of being the only component left that engages in independent work. The Murphy firm's interiors department was spun out years before as Interiors Incorporated, one of several subsidiary companies owned by the Murphys. After a few years it ran into trouble, dropping ultimately from 40 people to a staff of three. These last three were then folded into Murphy/Jahn and Interiors Incorporated was shut down. During the design phases of the firm's earliest speculative highrises, Jahn and the design teams worked out the lobbies as part of the package. But since interiors people are again on staff—headed by Nada Anderic, they consult on the interiors of the firm's projects such as the new Murphy/Jahn offices or the public floors of the Bank of the Southwest Tower as well as working for their own clients. Deborah Lampe Jahn, who was an interior designer with the firm when she met and later married Helmut, has been in charge of interiors for several projects and now has her own firm.

In 1983, with Charles Murphy Sr. long retired and his sons developing other interests, first Robert and then Charles Jr. made buy-out arrangements that left Jahn uncontestably in charge of the firm. It was the first time he had agreed to own any part of the operation. When offered stock in the past, he responded that he was only interested in buying into the firm if he could buy 51 percent. Now that he is in the position of making such decisions, Jahn is increasingly under pressure to make stock available to his associates. It is a ticklish dilemma for him. There are managerial advantages of including the top people and corporate disadvantages of being forced to buy back stock at inopportune times should anyone leave. Jahn watched from the sidelines as a faltering C. F. Murphy Associates had to find the capital to make it possible for Summers to leave.

This is, however, certain to be only the first of many such decisions. Jahn spent the last decade consolidating his position within the firm, remolding the firm to suit both the times and his tastes and, finally, inheriting complete control. Significantly, this is the first time in a history extending back 111 years, that a man predominantly interested in designing has headed the firm. Jahn's demonstrated business acumen and keen but tractable competitiveness have guided the firm out of its difficulty and into completely new directions. The next decades will, perforce, involve him in decisions that will determine the nature of the succession.

BUILDINGS AND PROJECTS

R. CROSBY KEMPER SR. MEMORIAL ARENA

KANSAS CITY, MO.
Design begun 1973,
construction completed 1974.

The first major building to come out of the firm with Jahn's name distinctly attached to it, the Kemper Arena established his reputation as an adventurous designer and linked it to space age technology. The three giant trusses, that hold the roof in suspension above and independent from the tiers of seats and support spaces below, serve both a practical function in allowing a fast-tracking of construction that produced the building in under 18 months and an aesthetic purpose in investing an enormously bulky and closed building with considerable visual romance.

Designed for flexibility, the arena seats up to 18,000 people at hockey games, basketball, track events, boxing, music programs, livestock shows and conventions.

The two tiers of seating are part of a concrete substructure. The metal walls and roof, suspended from giant trusses, form the superstructure. The two elements are independent. The three exterior trusses, that give the 325- by 424-foot interior a column-free enclosure, are made of standard tube varying between 30 and 48 inches in diameter and ⅜ to 1¼ inches thick is bolted together with internal tube stiffeners. The trusses are 27 feet deep and set 153 feet on center. The substructure takes no vertical loads from the roof or exterior wall. Loads from the trusses are transferred to steel hangers angled out from the building, leading to pin connections that sit on concrete piles driven 60 feet into the earth. Inside, directly beneath the tubular truss, are cantilevered roof trusses that allow the secondary frame span to be reduced to 45 feet.

The arena was designed on the oval plan rather than a circular one in order to bring more seats closer to the center and to reduce the required span of the super-structure by 76 feet. Entrances are at concourse level, with an equal number of seats above and below. Excess excavation permitted a berm around the building providing a walkway at concourse level. Four mechanical rooms for air conditioning, at the corners of the upper level, provide canopies over the spectator entrances by creating a rectangle, superimposed on the oval below.

The exterior wall consists of insulated metal panels, painted white. Interior partitions are concrete block. Technical and structural elements are left exposed and painted bright colors, and the finishes, including seating, are various shades of blue.

1. Side elevation
2. Corner detail

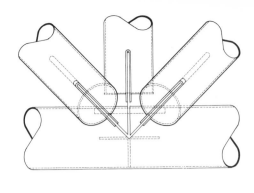

3. Construction details of roof trusses
4. Framing diagram
5. Overall view
6. Truss detail
7. Roof level detail

3

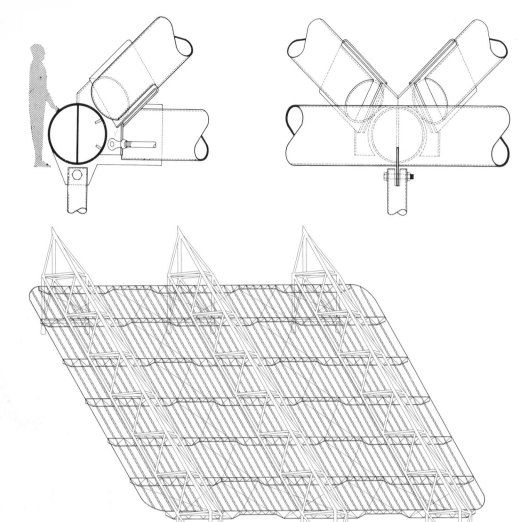

4

5

LEARNING RESOURCES CENTER, AURARIA HIGHER EDUCATION CENTER

DENVER, CO.
Design begun 1974,
construction completed 1976.

The library uses inexpensive, relatively low technology to reduce energy costs and an open plan to provide flexibility for the three higher education institutions—a community college, state college and state university—who share the downtown Denver campus. Two-foot-deep mechanical sunshades, set at 40 degree angles, shield the southern and western elevations from the mile-high city's fierce sun but allow some solar gain during winter months when the sun's rays penetrate at lower angles. Natural light provides forty percent of the building's daytime requirements and highly efficient metal halide fixtures are used for the remainder. There is cross ventilation through operable windows, rather than air-conditioning, with fan rooms located at the perimeter of each level. A system of multiple fans provide flexible use and fin-tube radiation at the perimeter allows fans to be turned off when the library is unoccupied. The thin extruded aluminum frame of the exterior, insulated metal panels and sun-

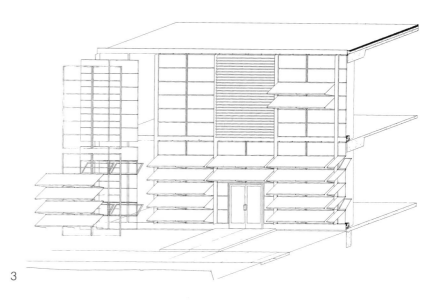

3

shades are factory finished in a white acrylic enamel to reflect sunlight.

The interior is open loft space in which the only fixed elements are two courtyards and three open concrete stairways. The landscaped courtyards, set asymmetrically within the rectangle, provide light and air to the interior as well as outdoor patios. Some interior partitions are accented in bright primary colors, and exposed fixtures and ducts are painted silver gray. A 20,000-square-foot partial basement houses a media facility. The building has a total square footage of 184,000.

The structure is a one-way system of cast-in-place concrete with post-tensioned beams and joints supported by round columns at 30-foot intervals. The exterior curtainwall is entirely independent of concrete work. Transparent glass, metal panels and mechanical louvers within the modular frame are arranged according to the angle of the sun and the varying functional needs inside.

1. Ceiling partition relationship, vertical dimensions, skin system, skin details, and corner details
2. Corner detail
3. Axonometric section of wall
4. Site plan
5. Elevation and section

4

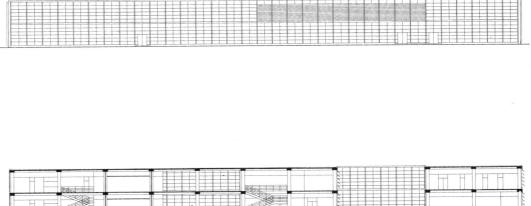

5

6

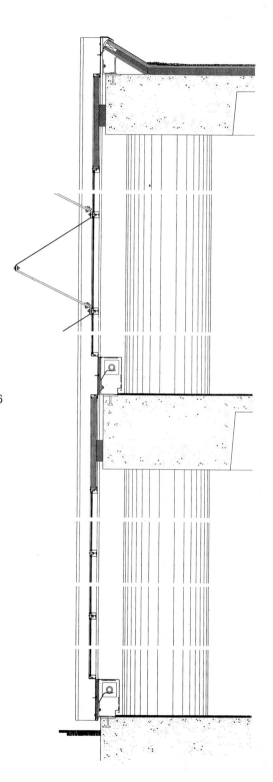

7

8

10

6. Wall detail
7. View looking towards interior courtyard
8,9. Curtain wall sections
10. Entrance detail
11. Interior detail showing sun shades

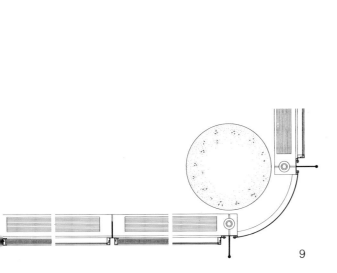

9

11

FOURTH DISTRICT COURTS BUILDING

MAYWOOD, IL.
Design begun 1974,
construction completed 1976.

The long, linear loft-style building (440 feet long by 140 feet wide), in a suburb west of Chicago, houses ten courtrooms with ancillary spaces and also a number of county offices. The courts requiring the greatest public access are located at ground level, with offices, a law library and staff lounges above. A basement level provides space for secure detention of the accused. The visitor enters, off-center, into a double-height lobby leading to a double-height internal "street," which runs along the whole front of the building and down each end. This corridor, punctuated by ficus trees, also acts as an additional sound buffer between the courts and a nearby expressway.

A straightforward steel structure of rigid frames with three lines of columns set 50 feet apart and cantilevered a further 20 feet at each end provides column-free space for the courtrooms in the center. The smaller bays house mainly offices. The exterior wall is composed of 10-foot by 32-foot units of rolled steel sections, designed to carry the live load deflections of the cantilever. The long walls are completely glazed in a gasket system, and the end walls, anticipated slightly by the corner modules of the long sides, express clearly differentiated stories. All the steel is painted a deep plum color.

1. Double-height entrance building
2. Entrance detail
3. Overall view
4. Ground floor plan

1

2

4th District Circuit Court Building

3

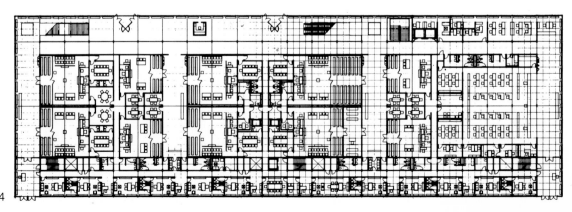

4

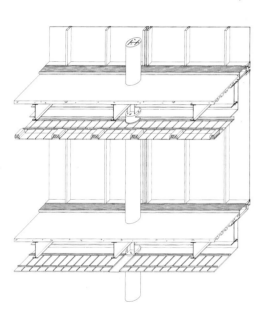

JOHN MARSHALL COURTS BUILDING

RICHMOND, VA.
Design begun 1973,
construction completed 1976.

Named for the historic John Marshall House that shares its site, the 137,000-square-foot municipal courts building fits into a complex of city and federal government buildings. The building takes the form of a parallelogram at ground level to facilitate pedestrian shortcuts within the complex. Above, the floors are rectangular, taking full advantage of the plot and providing canopies for the pedestrian paths and entry plaza beneath. Within, visitors use public corridors, while an easily secured private corridor system serves the judges' chambers, offices and protected entrances to the courts. Detainees awaiting trial are kept apart and transported by elevator directly to the criminal courts.

Regular 40-foot bays permit the large courtrooms to be column-free. The glass and steel building sits on a base faced in red brick, which is continued as paving for the landscaped plaza. All exterior glass is tinted bronze.

1. Overall view
2. Axonometric/section
3. Corner detail

1

2

MICHIGAN CITY PUBLIC LIBRARY

MICHIGAN CITY, IN.
Design begun 1974,
construction completed 1977.

Set in the declining center of an industrial town, the 32,280-square-foot library is sheathed in translucent insulated fiberglass panels, with a clear glass edge only for the entry bay. Diffuse light enters through these walls but basically the perfectly square building opens upward through a sawtooth series of clerestory windows set on the diagonal to capture north light. The insulated panels, extensive reliance on natural light and zipped aluminum insulated roof panels result in a high degree of energy efficiency. The two grids are developed to give a certain design complexity to what is essentially flexible loft space. At roof level, all permanent elements—structure, enclosure, ductwork and lights—follow the diagonal grid of the clerestories, while the walls and furnishings follow the rectilinear grid. Set asymmetrically within the building is a perfectly square garden court with trees and seats for outdoor reading. Its clear glass walls allow for more natural light inside.

Offices with low partitions occupy the perimeter. Reading and stack areas are defined by movable furniture. Only the meeting/lecture rooms are separated by full-height walls. The floor is completely carpeted in a yellow, diagonally striped pattern. Exposed mechanical supply equipment is bright green with exhaust hardware painted bright blue. All exposed structure is white, and the furniture is finished in yellow and various shades of blue.

3

1. Front elevation
2. Front elevation at dusk
3. Ground floor plan
4. Isometric/framing drawing

4

5

5. Entrance
6. Reading area facing courtyard

6

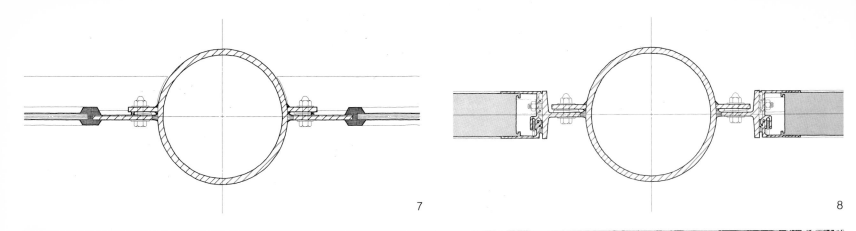

7

8

9

7,8. Wall details
9. View showing clerestory windows
10. Sketches
11. Study carols lit by translucent wall
12. Interior

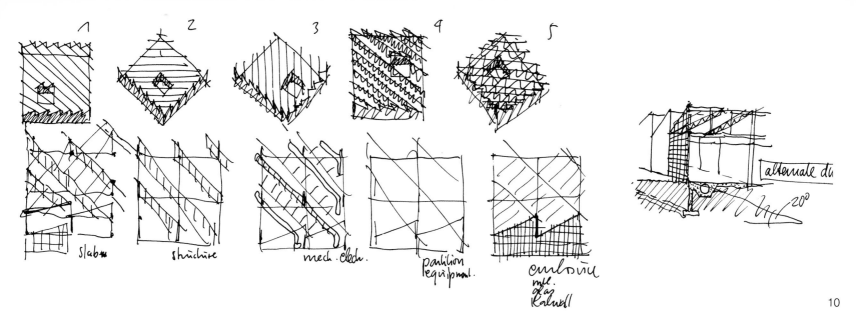

1   2   3   4   5

slab   structure   mech. elec.   partition / equipment.   enclosure mil. glas Kalwall

alternate du

20°

1

DE LA GARZA CAREER CENTER

EAST CHICAGO, IN.
Design begun 1975,
construction completed 1981.

The 106,000-square-foot vocational training center and its parking lot occupy six acres between an industrial section and a deteriorated neighborhood in a poor community. The long-span structure provides a central circulation spine with two stories of classrooms on one side and double-height, double-span workshops on the other. The long spans are created by a standard structure of trusses, girders and joists on pipe columns. The exterior wall is press-formed steel sash and insulated panels with gasketed glass. The structure is suppressed on long sides, exposed at ends.

Bright color enlivens the building both inside and out. The aluminum curtainwall frame and infill metal panels are two shades of bright yellow. The green exposed columns and plate girders contrast with blue mechanical systems and the door frames, garage doors and flagpole which are orange.

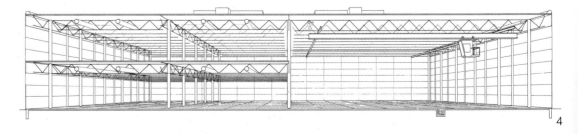

3

4

1. Back elevation
2. Wall detail
3. Mechanical plant
4. Section/perspective
5. Mechanical plant detail 5

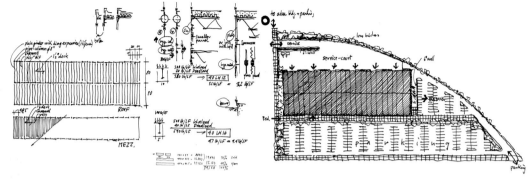

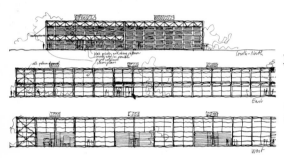

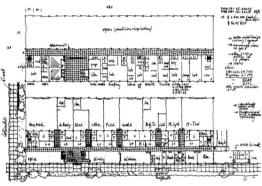

6

7

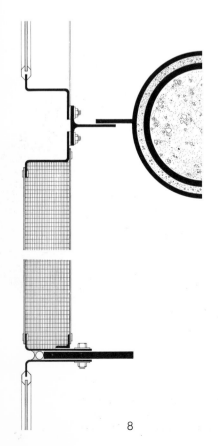

8

9

44

ABU DHABI CONFERENCE CITY

Competition Entry.
UNITED ARAB EMIRATES.
Designed in 1975.

Located on a narrow peninsula in the Arabian Gulf where midday temperatures regularly reach 120 degrees Fahrenheit, the projected city is linear, strung along a landscaped skylit spine, and buried 90 feet below grade. Visitors enter the 4860-foot-long by only 270-foot-wide city from a grade parking lot at one end. The president's residence stands underneath at the near end; at the far end, the spine culminates in a five-story conference center, projecting above ground. In between, the spine is divided into two levels of circulation, separated for people and services, the lower one designed as a tropical garden. The skylit corridor is shaded by large movable screens on the southern edge, which also serves as a major art project, representing the various landscapes of the world. Thirty guest houses for kings, heads of state and delegates are grouped in pairs along the spine between the center and the president's house. Movable screens and glass walls allow visitors the desired degree of openness or privacy within each house.

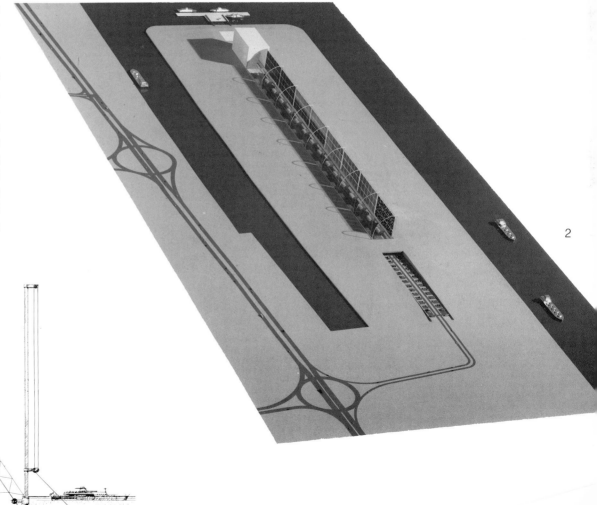

1

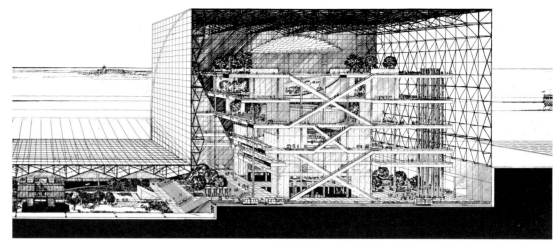

2

3

1. Section/perspective looking north
2. Overall view, conceptual model
3. Section/perspective looking east

46

1

ST. MARY'S ATHLETIC FACILITY

NOTRE DAME, IN.
Design begun 1976,
construction completed 1977.

A bright, sunny, open gymnasium is created with a long-span structural system wrapped in a thin membrane of translucent and transparent materials. The 42,000-square-foot facility contains two floors of racquetball courts, lounge, faculty offices and lobby at one end and a low bay area for gymnastics, fencing and dance at the other. Between is a double-height playing floor for basketball, tennis and other sports. Demountable bleachers, seating 1800, fold into the walls. The building is also used for social events and official assemblies at the small women's college.

Sunk half a level into the ground and surrounded by an earth berm, the two-level building appears lower and its bulk on the campus is reduced. The berm also reduces heat loss from the building in severe winter weather. Visitors enter at the gallery level, where bright red structure, blue pipes and mustard yellow ducts provide a colorful interaction in the upper reaches. Certain interior partitions and the trophy case pick up the palette below. Outside, the wall is composed of white panels of insulated translucent fiberglass, the outer layer of which is rippled, within a red aluminum frame. Glass interrupts at the entry and the edges of each end. Above, a curved clerestory of clear acrylic fills the interior with light as it softens the shape of the rectangle.

The structural system is exposed steel with prefabricated trusses spanning 120 feet with 20-foot spacing, cantilevered 7 feet 6 inches at each end. Ground face "soundblock" on the sidewalls of the playing floor and the acoustic deck help with sound absorption. Flooring in the gym areas is polyurethane surfacing, with carpet and unsealed concrete elsewhere.

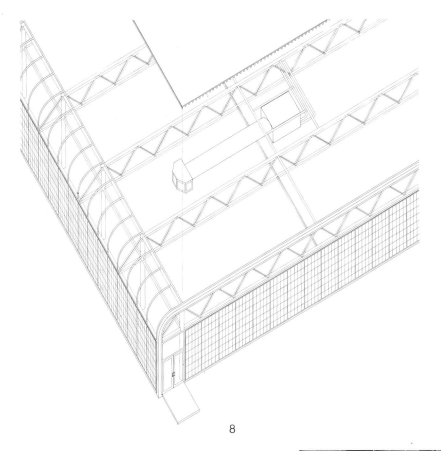

8

9

8. Axonometric section showing framing system
9. Ceiling detail
10. Volleyball court
   Overleaf:
11,12. Interior views

10

11

12

5,6. Interior looking across atrium
7. Exterior at dusk
8. Underground parking level, entry level plan,
   and second level plan
9. Section/perspective
10. Overall view

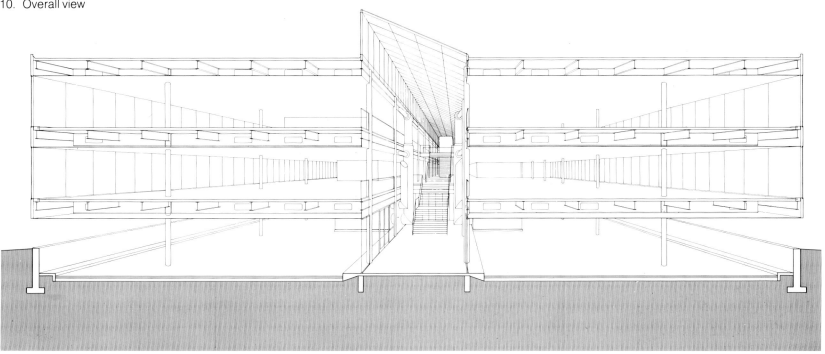

9

0

PARKING GARAGE

SPRINGFIELD, IL.
Design begun 1977,
construction completed 1979.

Designed as the first phase of a garage/ hotel complex, the 750-car garage serves an adjacent convention center and includes a skylit walkway to the center and the street. The 264,000-square-foot parking structure has six levels, two of which are underground, at heights consistent with the planned hotel.

The longitudinal circulation spine has arched skylights with red trim and steel press-formed exterior wall panels with blue guard rails. Stairs and natural ventilation shafts are located within. Automobile ramps continue as bridges through the spine. The 65-foot by 25-foot structural bay accommodates 90-degree parking stalls without interference from columns. The superstructure is a precast concrete longspan girder and short span Triple-Tee system. A below-grade shell is provided by reinforced concrete foundation walls, footings and floor slab.

1. Stairwell detail
2. Overall view

1

2

LA LUMIERE GYMNASIUM

LA PORTE, WI.
Design begun 1977,
construction completed 1978.

A low-cost gymnasium for a small private school uses an off-the-shelf bowstring arch closed at each end with glass curtainwall and a sunken playing floor to provide the necessary height with the least amount of exterior skin. The arch is a double shell stressed skin system of corrugated thin-gauge galvanized metal. Between the shells are two inches of fiberglass insulation and the inner shell is perforated to absorb sound. Lighting tubes are fitted into the roof's corrugation to provide some protection against wayward balls. Operable windows in the end walls provide natural ventilation. Free-standing cores contain lockers and showers.

1. Side elevation
2. Front elevation
3. End wall details
4. Interior

1

2

3

4

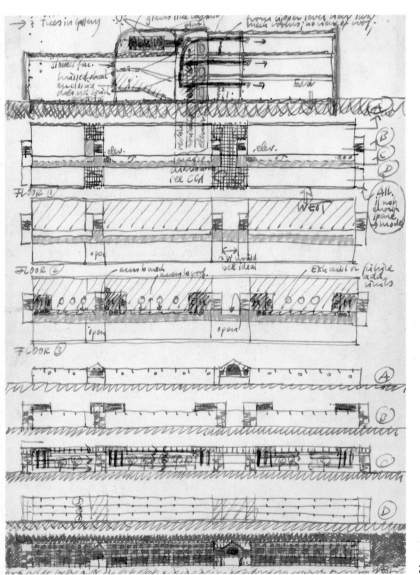

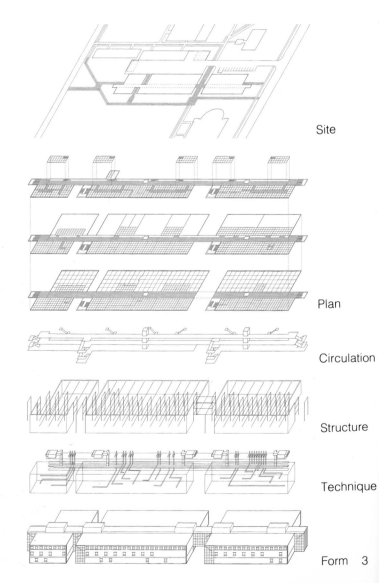

Site

Plan

Circulation

Structure

Technique

Form

2

3

AGRICULTURAL ENGINEERING SCIENCES BUILDING, UNIVERSITY OF ILLINOIS

CHAMPAIGN-URBANA, IL.
Design begun 1978,
construction completed 1983.

The lab and classroom building attempts to unify a chaotic area south of the main campus quadrangle by shoring up a new quadrangle and by using some of the materials and forms of the original Neo-Georgian campus. The wall-like building, which forms the eastern edge of a new south quadrangle envisioned in the university's masterplan, actually consists of three linear buildings, laid end-to-end. They house the forestry, agricultural engineering and food sciences departments of the College of Agriculture and are connected by a continuous enclosed "street" that runs through the center of all three buildings. At one intersection, the connection exists only on the second level, in order to preserve a favorite pedestrian route across campus.

While the design is not within the Georgian tradition itself, as indicated by the asymmetrical and irregular window pattern and the prefabricated metal panels and glass curtainwalls, traditional elements are deliberately woven into the elevations. The long sides have brick walls and punched windows with heads and sills, like the older university buildings. These brick surfaces are divided by string courses and the brick corners are embellished with quoining. Sections of modern curtainwall appear unexpectedly and deliberately contrast with the rhythms, texture, color, scale and patterning of the brick wall.

The steel frames for the 106,000-square-foot building are set 20 feet apart with the cross-section span varying from 15 feet for the circulation "street" to 30 feet for classrooms and 50 feet for laboratories.

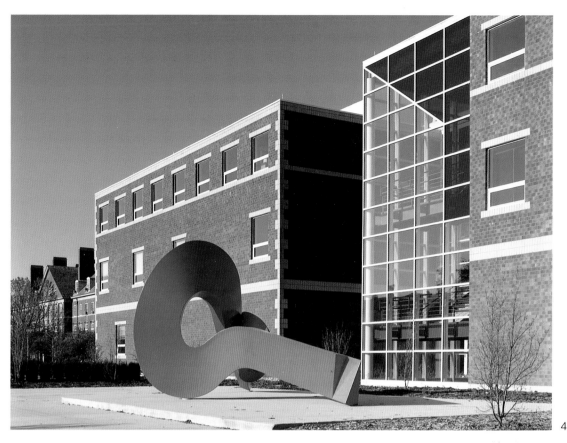

4

5

6

Preceding pages:
1. Front elevation
2. Sketches
3. Schematic diagrams
4. Sculpture at main entrance
5. Contextual photo

6. Stair detail
7. End detail
8. Dock/loading facilities

7

FIRST SOURCE CENTER

SOUTH BEND, IN.
Design begun 1978,
construction completed 1981
(hotel), 1982 (bank).

Two rectangular blocks—a 150,000-square-foot, eight-story bank and office building and a 300-room, nine-story hotel—are linked by a web of intersecting glass walls and trusses forming a prismatic, 27,000-square-foot atrium between them. The atrium provides a grand entry hall for both buildings; with their elevators pulled out into the space and glass-enclosed for drama from within and animation from without. The hotel restaurant spreads out under the glass canopy in the manner of a European street cafe.

Both buildings are of reinforced concrete with varying bay sizes. The floors of the hotel are load-bearing masonry with prestressed precast slabs. On the atrium sides the exterior walls are striped in aluminum, gray, clear and silver glass with aluminum and gray glass facing the street. The glass canopy over the atrium alternates clear and silver bands. Two levels of parking are provided below grade.

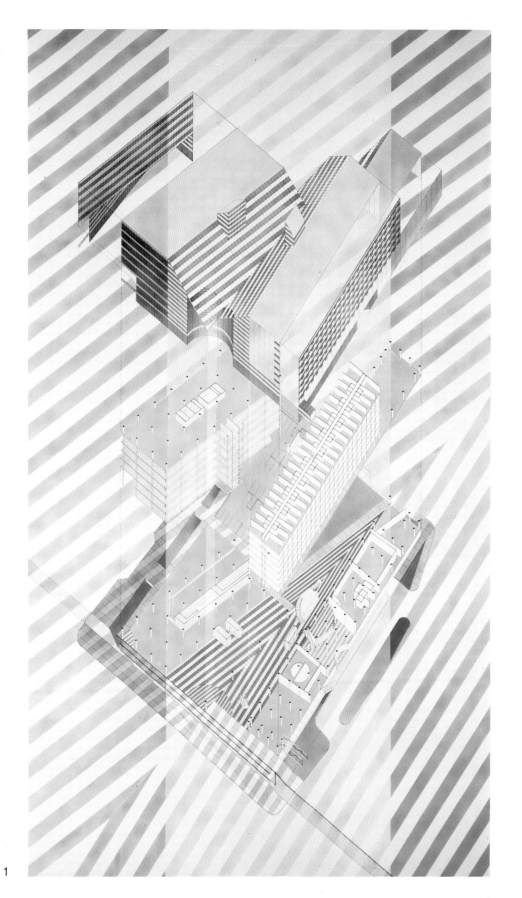

1. Pull-apart axonometric airbrush rendering
   Overleaf:
2. Front elevation, principal entry
3. Entry at night
4. Atrium above hotel
5. View looking towards main entry
6. Hotel restaurant/atrium space
7. Interior atrium

1

3

4

64

8

9

10

8. Bank lobby
9. Bank entrance
10. Rear elevation

DISTRICT HEADQUARTERS, COMMONWEALTH EDISON COMPANY

BOLINGBROOK, IL.
Design begun 1978,
construction completed 1981.

The front building houses offices for administering nearby utility construction and for public relations. The back building is used for storage and vehicle maintenance. They are linked visually by the use of similar materials and a shared axis, and are designed to be linked physically if additional space is desired later.

As Commonwealth Edison has made energy conservation a major element of its public relations and company policy, materials enclosing the building are highly efficient: insulation-backed aluminum corrugated siding, insulation-backed spandrel glass, double-glazed gray-tinted windows and roof insulation. Thermal storage systems reduce energy demands during peak cooling loads by making ice at night for daytime use. In addition, the substructure of the maintenance and storage building acts as a heat sink and the electric water heaters are assisted by solar panels.

The structural system consists of spread footings and concrete slabs on grade, a steel cantilevered roof, and pipe columns, rolled sections and open web joists. The typical bay size is 20 feet by 25 feet. Diagonal bracing is used for the maintenance and storage building.

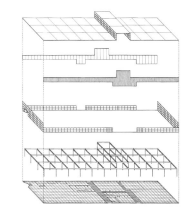
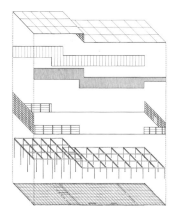

1

2

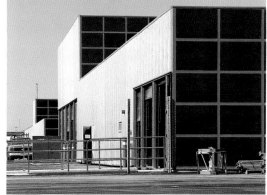

3

4

1. Axonometric pull-apart framing drawings
2. Relationship between the customer services building and the vehicle maintenance facility
3. Interior, vehicle maintenance facility
4. Exterior, vehicle maintenance facility

ARGONNE PROGRAM SUPPORT FACILITY

ARGONNE NATIONAL LABORATORIES, IL.
Design begun 1978,
construction completed 1982.

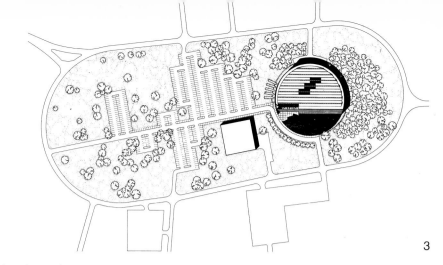

3

The 215,000-square-foot building, serving both the famous scientific laboratory and the Chicago branch of the Department of Energy, was intended as a virtual demonstration project for energy-conserving design. Its overall shape is a conscious symbol of the sun, the circle being made up of the building and the retention point next to it. The curved corners lower the building's surface-to-area ratio, reducing heat loss and gain through the perimeter. Among the other energy-saving devices are louvered awnings facing south that shield windows on that side from summer sun while allowing lower-angled winter light and reflected light from the pool of water through. Originally the angled frame that holds the louvers was to have held solar collectors while the pond was introduced to reflect lost rays back onto them.

Fundamental to the design is the contention that using natural light provides savings that far outweigh any heat loss or gain through glass. Sixty-five percent of required light is provided by the ribbons of windows that encircle the exterior and the staggered skylights over double- and triple-height atria. Supplemental fluorescent lighting is turned on and off automatically by sensors reading the light level and task lighting is provided at work stations. The interior plan is open in order to distribute light and air with the least duplication of equipment and light is borrowed from perimeter offices through clerestory glazing in interior partitions. Surplus heat generated during the day is stored in water tanks buried in the ground for use at night. In the summer, water is chilled during off-peak hours to take advantage of less expensive energy.

For the most part, the structure is a standard 30-foot-bay steel system with metal decks and concrete floors, with the steel columns filled with concrete for fireproofing and full penetration welds joining several girders to columns for stiffening. The S-curved entry wall, however, uses a four-plate serpentine box girder.

Colors on both interior and exterior are limited to white, silver and green with decorative checkerboard patterns for both the entry wall—in aluminum panels and green-framed windows—and the wall-to-wall carpeting in two shades of green.

1. Aerial view
2. Front elevation
3. Site plan
4. View looking northeast with sun shades on south
5. End wall detail

4

5

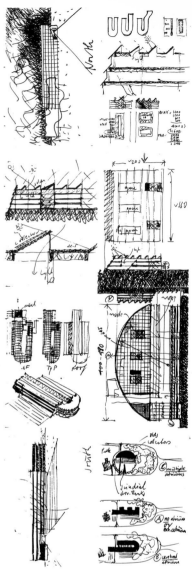

6. Entrance detail
7. Sketches
8. Elevation detail

7

CHICAGO BOARD OF TRADE ADDITION

CHICAGO, IL.
Design begun 1978,
construction completed 1982.
In joint venture with
Shaw and Associates and Swanke,
Hayden & Connell Architects.

The Chicago Board of Trade building by Holabird & Root, 1980, is celebrated not only for its landmark design but for its prominent position visually ending the city's traditional financial street. The client's desire for an addition that would establish a relationship to the landmark led first to a design based on the scalloped ornament in its lobby but magnified as a scallop-shaped building. The clients' rejection of this as insufficiently literal led to the final design, a smaller, abstracted, space age translation of the landmark set immediately behind it and adjoining at lobby and trading floor level. The salient characteristics of the original building—setbacks, hip roof, tripartite vertical composition, finial, the clock above the door—are reproduced but transformed in the 634,000-square-foot addition. Walls of limestone with punched windows are translated into a taut membrane of mirror glass that slips behind limestone screen walls on the sides. The setbacks are fewer and flatter with tall inserts of black glass providing a vertical rhythm analogous to the recesses and windows of the original. An octagon-shaped roof ornament corresponds to the statue of Ceres above the existing landmark. The octagon, the logo of the Exchange, repeats the shape of the building's original trading pits.

At the base, the sides project 20 feet beyond the original building to provide a wider trading floor but at ground level it keeps the narrower gauge creating arcaded walkways on east and west elevations. The walkways are flanked with red and green columns and covered in a green plaster canopy. There are entrances from both walkways for convenience and a formal entry from the south, across from that of the existing tower, leading into the lobby

through an arcade flanked by ground and mezzanine level shops. The scallop-shaped ornament that had originally been thought of as a design for the whole building is used throughout the interior as a decorative motif. At the doorway, it appears as a theater curtain-style entry arch, and elsewhere in furniture, flooring and the shape of the mezzanine.

The first twelve floors of the building contain a three-story trading floor and support spaces for the commodities market, which is designed to function with the original building as one unit. Beginning at floor twelve, it becomes an office building wrapped in a U-shape around a twelve-story skylit atrium. The adjacent wall of the original tower provides the fourth edge of the atrium. Glass elevators within the space carry passengers to the balcony corridors of upper floors. Paving, light fixtures and balconies are also elaborated with scalloped shapes and patterns in a palette of blue-greens. A major focal point is a 60-foot-tall canvas mural that was rescued from a closet and restored. The mural had once adorned the trading room of the original building but was removed when that room was double-decked.

The structural system supports the small-bayed office building above without interrupting the trading floors with columns by using the floors immediately below the skylobby for two-story-deep trusses. The trussed space also houses mechanical equipment for the building.

4

5

6

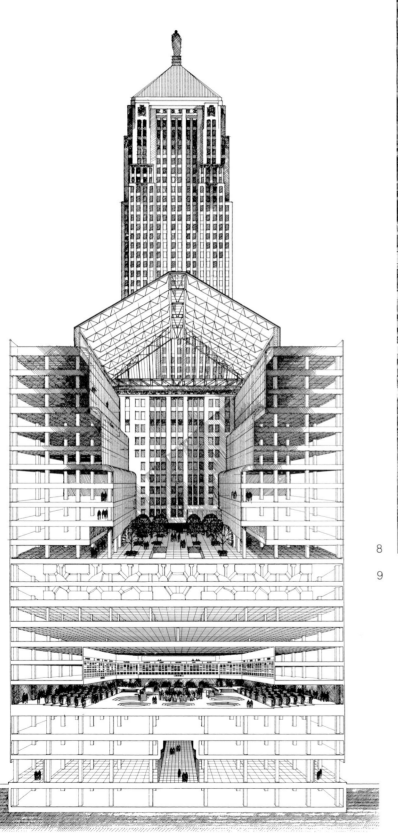

8

9

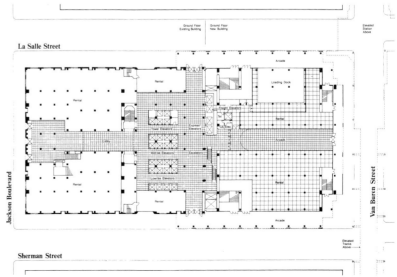

CBOT trading floor

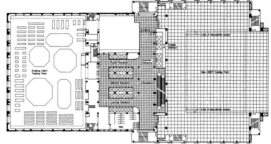

Skylobby

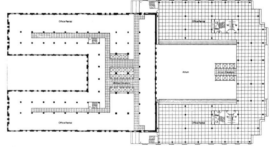

18 & 19 office floors

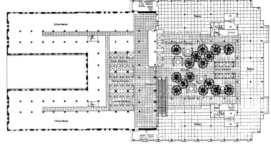

3

4

15

16

17

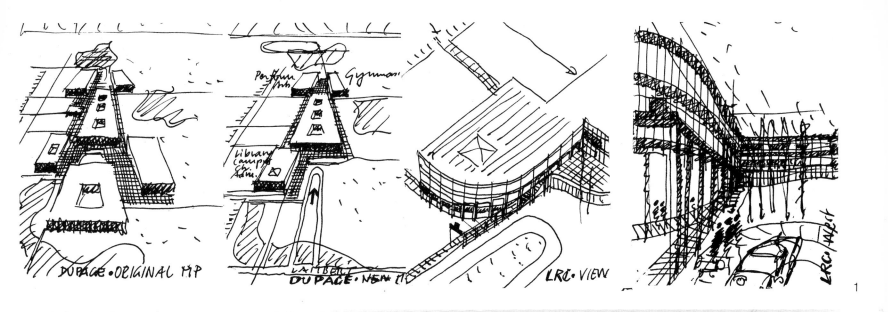

COLLEGE OF DU PAGE LEARNING RESOURCES CENTER

GLEN ELLYN, IL.
Design begun 1979,
construction completed 1983.

The building consolidates a variety of functions that were formerly located in temporary facilities throughout the new campus. The exterior materials of the only other permanent facility—reflective glass and weathering steel—are picked up in the new building. The library, occupying the top floor, is lit by a series of skylights. The middle level, which can be entered directly from the plaza, contains school administration offices. A student center, cafeteria and bookstore occupy the arcaded perimeter of the lowest level, with a kitchen and mechanical spaces along the edge built into the slope.

1. Design sketches
2. Overall view with addition at left

3. West corner detail
4. View looking towards cafeteria
5. Overall view
6. Interior main staircase looking towards existing building
7. Exterior main staircase looking towards new addition
8. Exterior main staircase

1

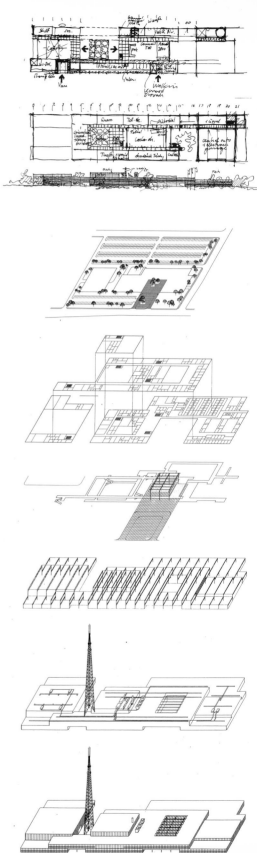

2

AREA 2 POLICE HEADQUARTERS

CHICAGO, IL.
Design begun 1977,
construction completed 1982.

The 135,000 square feet of diverse law enforcement functions—police station, detention facility, vehicle maintenance shop, courts and sheriff's station—take various shapes and sizes as their needs dictate but are unified by the palette of materials and an arrangement that wraps the different elements around a common courtyard. On the exterior, materials include insulated metal panels inset with windows of vandal-resistent glass block. Visitors to the police station or the courts enter through the courtyard under a sculpture by Loren Madsen, consisting of 700 translucent acrylic blocks, suspended from the roof by stainless steel cables. Lobbies off this protected area are separated by glass walls to project an image of accessibility.

In addition to the symbolic blue of the exterior, bright colors distinguish columns, stairs and mechanical systems. The structural system responds to changing configurations with frames of varying length, set 30 feet apart. Energy conservation is promoted by a highly efficient building envelope and reliance on natural light in perimeter areas.

1. Courtyard sculpture with tower in background
2. Cut-away perspective section
3. Design sketches
4. Systems drawings
5. View looking north
6. Curtain wall detail

7. View looking southeast
8. Glass block enclosed stairs
9. Police vehicle maintenance garage

8

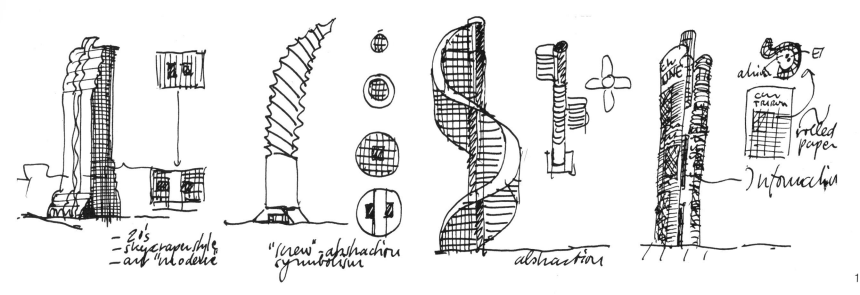

CHICAGO TRIBUNE TOWER

Late Competition Entry.
Designed in 1979.

Two fellow Chicago architects and an art dealer staged a "Late Entries to the Chicago Tribune Tower Competition" exhibit that elicited 90 submissions from architects all over the world. The exhibit rules specified that the drawing be of a skyscraper, playing off the legendary 1922 competition for the headquarters of the Chicago newspaper. There was, however, no program, no winner and no commission. Helmut Jahn's entry is a play on the 1922 winner, a building that has long been a landmark in Chicago. Jahn's drawing depicts the tower, in all its Gothic glory, surmounted by the shell of a contemporary glass version as if the glass sheath had just been pulled up and the masonry tower revealed underneath. Jahn accompanied his drawing with these words: "The image of this skyscraper pursues an appropriate recomposition of classic and modern principles of the building arts. Through its new typology the building suggests how we can build for a future that honors its past, while above all expressing the truth of our contemporary condition."

1,2. Design sketches
3. Airbrush rendering

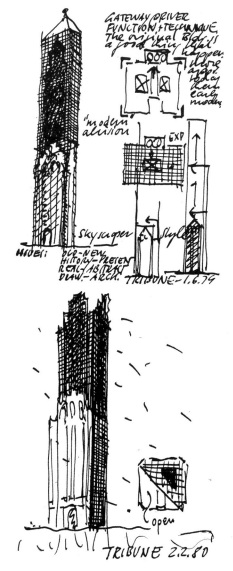

2

1

3

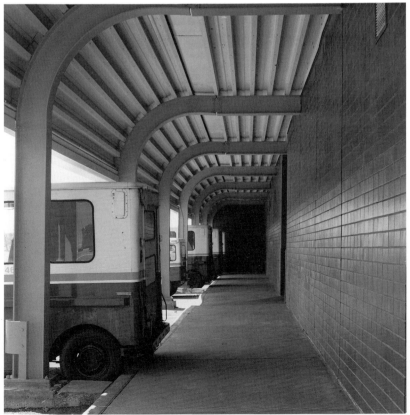

UNITED STATES POST OFFICE

OAK BROOK, IL.
Design begun 1979,
construction completed 1981.

The suburban post office takes its design cue from the equipment associated with the U.S. mails. The 21,000-square-foot rectangle is rounded on top like a mail box and colored red, white and blue like a mail truck. Its structural system is an exposed steel frame composed of 12-inch-deep wide flange members. Prefinished metal deck spans between the members of the roof and continues around the curve to serve as subframing for the side walls. Side and end walls are clad in tile.

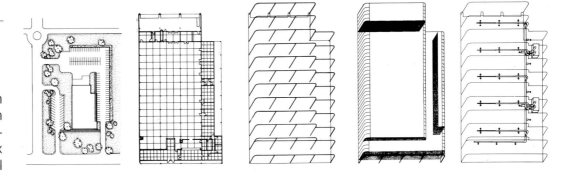

5

6

7

1. View looking west
2. Interior showing exposed structure
3. Corner detail, front facade
4. Sheltered delivery truck dock
5. Schematic diagrams
6. View looking northeast
7. View looking northwest

1

lights which increase in height as they approach the terminal. The concourse floors have an elaborate paving in several shades of terrazzo.

The roof framing of the terminal ticketing area is a "folded truss" system, which consists of pairs of steel trusses laid up at an angle to each other in order to take advantage of structural efficiencies inherent in folded plate structure. Typical bay sizes are 30 feet by 120 feet. The roof system for this area is metal roof anchored to metal deck and following the contour of the folded truss. The framing of the concourse faults are rolled steel sections, with its intermediate framing of steel tubes or rolled sections. The windbracing for the terminal and concourse areas is a combination of moment frames and braced cores.

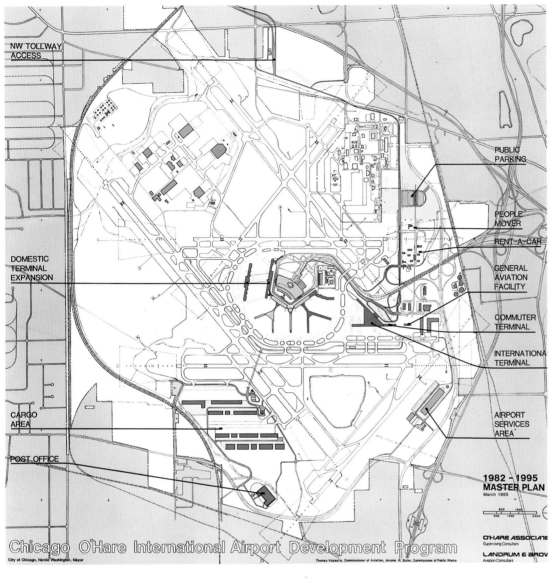

NW TOLLWAY ACCESS

PUBLIC PARKING

PEOPLE MOVER

RENT-A-CAR

DOMESTIC TERMINAL EXPANSION

GENERAL AVIATION FACILITY

COMMUTER TERMINAL

INTERNATIONAL TERMINAL

CARGO AREA

AIRPORT SERVICES AREA

POST OFFICE

1982 - 1995 MASTER PLAN
March 1985

Chicago O'Hare International Airport Development Program

City of Chicago, Harold Washington, Mayor

Thomas Kapsalis, Commissioner of Aviation, Jerome R. Butler, Commissioner of Public Works

O'HARE ASSOCIATE
Supervising Consultant

LANDRUM & BROW
Aviation Consultant

3

4

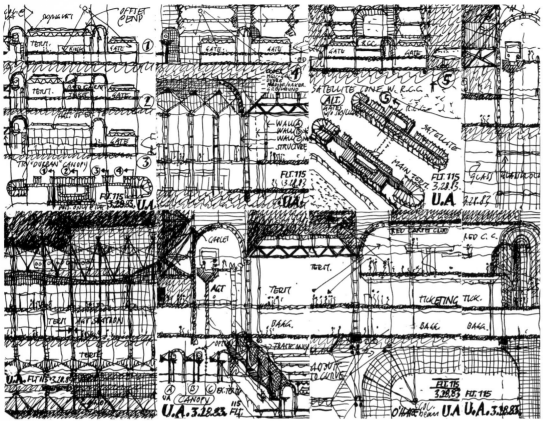

1

UNITED AIRLINES TERMINAL AND SATELLITE BUILDINGS

Chicago, Ill.
Construction: 1985–88

1. Sketches
2. Satellite departure gate facility
3. View towards end of satellite facility
4. Section/perspective
5. Covered connection between underground walkway and terminal
6. Detail of multi-level access to terminal
Overleaf:
7. Barrel-vaulted pedestrian spine
8. Section view of model
9. Pedestrian spine, escalators connecting to underground tunnel

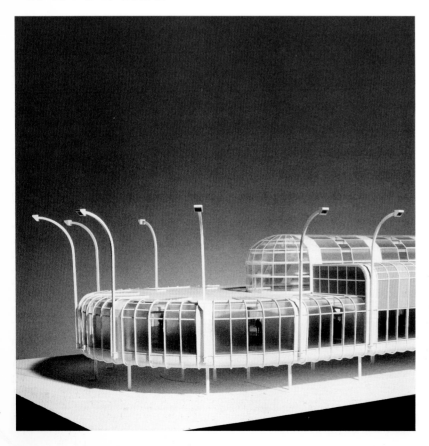

2

The new terminal and satellite buildings for United Airlines at O'Hare International Airport will provide 42 new gates and approximately 1,000,000 square feet of space for new holdrooms, concourses, ticketing areas, concessions, flight operations, and attendant facilities. Terminal and satellite buildings form parallel concourses, each 1,500 feet long, with an 815-foot separation allowing for dual taxiing of wide-body aircraft. The terminal portion contains an upper-level ticketing pavilion adjacent to the existing roadway. A barrel-vaulted circulation spine extends the length of the 16-gate concourse at the back of the pavilion, with holdrooms paralleling this spine. Flo-thru ticket counters create an open, expansive atmosphere in the ticketing pavilion. Natural light from skylights in the 120-foot free-span roof combines with "folded truss" steel superstructure and terrazzo floors to produce a carefully defined environment.

4

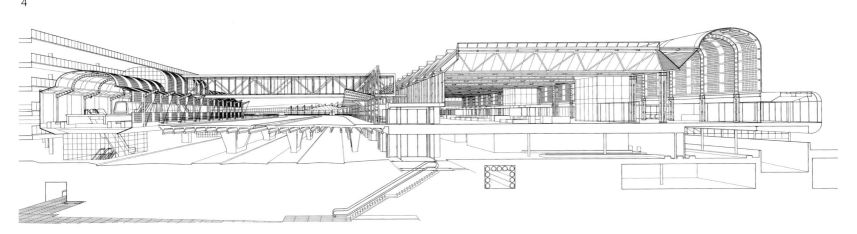

5

6

An underground pedestrian walkway, supplemented with moving walkways, links terminal facilities with the 26-gate satellite, which repeats the basic elements of the terminal building (barrel-vaulted spine and holdrooms), with a central area for ticketing, concessions, and flight operations.

1

1. Wall detail, tunnel
2. Underground pedestrian tunnel with moving sidewalks
3. Sketches

2

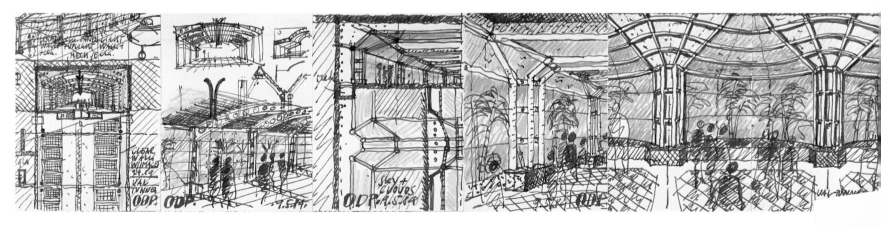

11 DIAGONAL STREET

JOHANNESBURG, SOUTH AFRICA.
Design begun 1981,
construction completed 1983.
In association with
Louis Karol Architects.

This 360,000-square-foot speculative office building is designed with a conscious allusion to the distribution of diamonds—a major business of the developer's parent company. The multidirectional cuts in the 20-story volume provide floors of varying size and conform efficiently to the sloping height restrictions imposed by the city's zoning ordinance. The building's glittering enclosure is actually a double skin. The outer wall is a silicone-glazed curtainwall in silver, blue and black reflective glass with occasional red trim. The glass is attached to aluminum frames with structural silicone prior to installation so that the frame is completely hidden from view. Its mirrored surfaces reduce heat gain from the extremely high solar radiation that penetrates Johannesburg's thin, clear air. The inner wall's glazing is arranged in continuous strips that are butt-joined and silicone-sealed. The mullionless glass allows complete visual flexibility in locating interior partitions along the exterior wall.

The exterior skin is cut away in a sawtooth pattern around most of the base of the building with more dramatic recesses behind the knife-edge descents of the curtainwall on both sides. In front, a full porte cochere is carved out behind the curtainwall. The five-story lobby is edged and covered in mirror-glass with a waterfall cascading down a sloping granite wall. There are two-story atriums on the top floor and above it two floors of penthouses with private elevators and wrap-around views of the city.

The structural system is reinforced concrete. The floor slabs are constructed with flying forms and the core with a slip form process. There are two below-grade levels with parking for 175 cars. The spine is illuminated at night.

1. Sketches
2. Johannesburg skyline
3. Cityscape
   Overleaf:
4. Night view of spire
5. Lobby with water fountain
6. Entrance
7. Contextual view
8. Detail of side elevation
9. Entrance
10. Front elevation

151

4

7

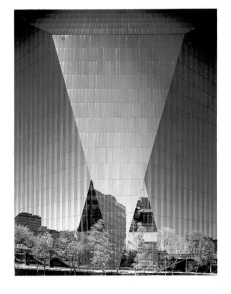

10

8

9

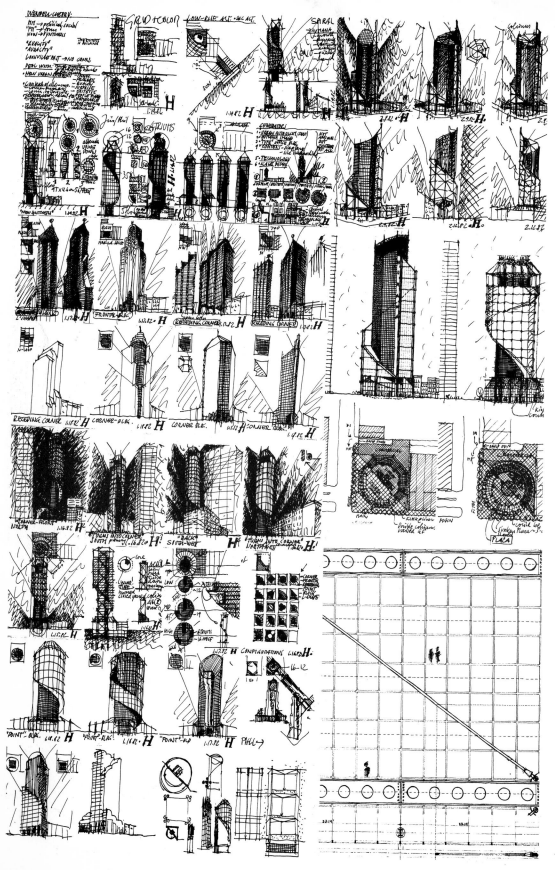

HUMANA, INC.

Competition Entry.
LOUISVILLE, KY.
Designed in 1982.

The firm's design for the headquarters of the international hospital management company was one of four runners-up but not the ultimate winner. In its design, an octagonal tower is wrapped in a spiraling outer shell of four-story atria that wind up and around its perimeter. The office floors are lifted six stories above the corner site, leaving a covered plaza on part of the site that is sunken three feet below the street level. Visitors enter through a wall that is articulated with exposed steel columns and subtle shadings of color intended to echo the character and scale of the historically significant cast iron buildings in the neighborhood. The entry leads to an interior arcade, used as an exhibit and cafe area, and onto the office lobby and a two-story commercial building at the south end of the site. Humana's executive suite is placed on the first office floor, with lounge and dining rooms in the lowest of the seven atria. A private elevator leads to a health club in the very top of the building which has a dramatically sloping eight-story lounge and reception area overlooking the Ohio River. The health center is shaped on the exterior as a recognizable crown, that would be identifiable on the Louisville skyline. Exterior materials are blue and silver reflective glass.

1. Sketches
2. Aerial model view
3. Views
4. Grand floor plan
5. Typical lowrise Humana office
6. Typical highrise tenant office

1

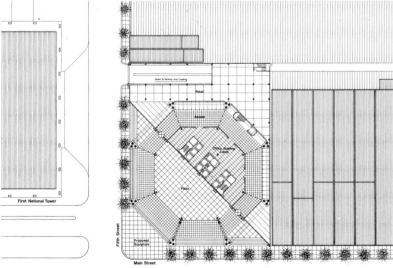

First National Tower

Fifth Street

Down To Parking And Loading

Retail

Arcade

Office, Building Lobby

Plaza

Proposed Sculpture

Main Street

American Life And Accident
Insurance Building

Place Montpelier

Kentucky Center For The Arts

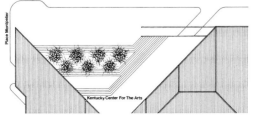
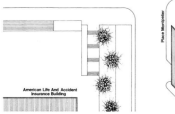

View of Executive Floor Atrium with Kentucky Arts Center and Ohio River beyond

View of Health Club Lounge with Ohio River beyond

View of Arcade with Lobby on left and Retail on right

3

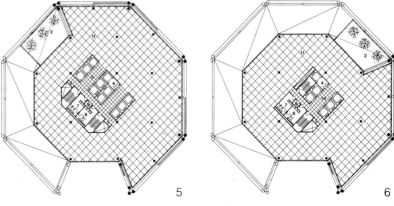

5

6

7. Contextual model view
8. Night rendering

EXPOSITION AND OFFICE COMPLEX

CHICAGO, IL.
Designed in 1981.

The plan is for five blocks of Chicago's downtown and includes 1.4 million square feet of exhibition space for computer products and one million square feet of commercial and retail development. The scallop-shaped exposition center occupies the area to one side of existing elevated railroad tracks with the commercial space on the other side. The existing cross-streets continue through the project on the ground level, but above, the buildings are linked together by a continuous galleria along the street front and a series of overhead bridges perpendicular to it. Cylindrical office towers are located on either side of each cross-street, punctuating the linear composition and marking each intersection with a symbolic gateway. The actual entrances to the galleria, however, are located in the middle of each block.

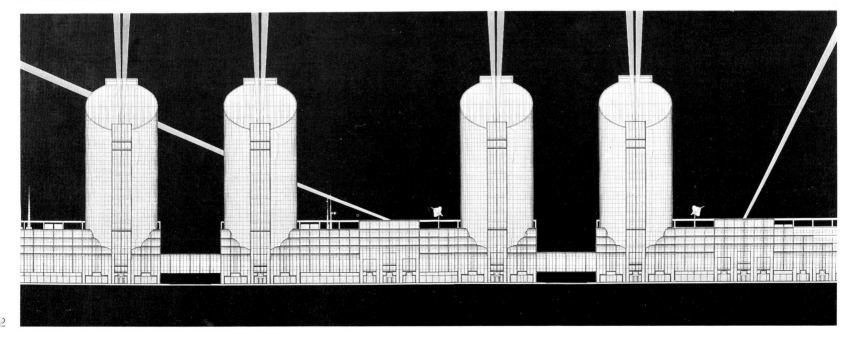

1. Sketches
2. Partial elevation

1

GREYHOUND TERMINAL

CHICAGO, IL.
Design begun 1982.

The design is an attempt to recreate the excitement and fantasy that was embodied in old-time railroad stations for a type of transportation whose image in America has been singularly utilitarian. Sculptured towers topped with spires mark each corner of the full-block site. Passengers enter under one of the spires and are whisked upstairs on escalators to a sunlit waiting area with a canopy modelled on nineteenth century garden conservatories. The building's site is in the midst of office towers and was therefore considered to have five facades: four all around and a fifth to be seen from windows above. Buses enter the building up a continuous ramp to docks arranged radially around the greenhouse-like waiting area. Facilities for the company's express package services, a restaurant, support facilities and customer parking are located on the ground level of the 250,000-square-foot terminal.

The side walls are reflective glass and the roof metal and glass to provide natural light, while louvers in the side walls permit natural ventilation. The structural system combines a steel superstructure and a concrete substructure.

1. Overall view of model
2. Corner detail
3. Section perspective
4. Model
5. Illuminated model showing bus ramp
   Overleaf:
6. Sketches
7. Plan/elevation rendering

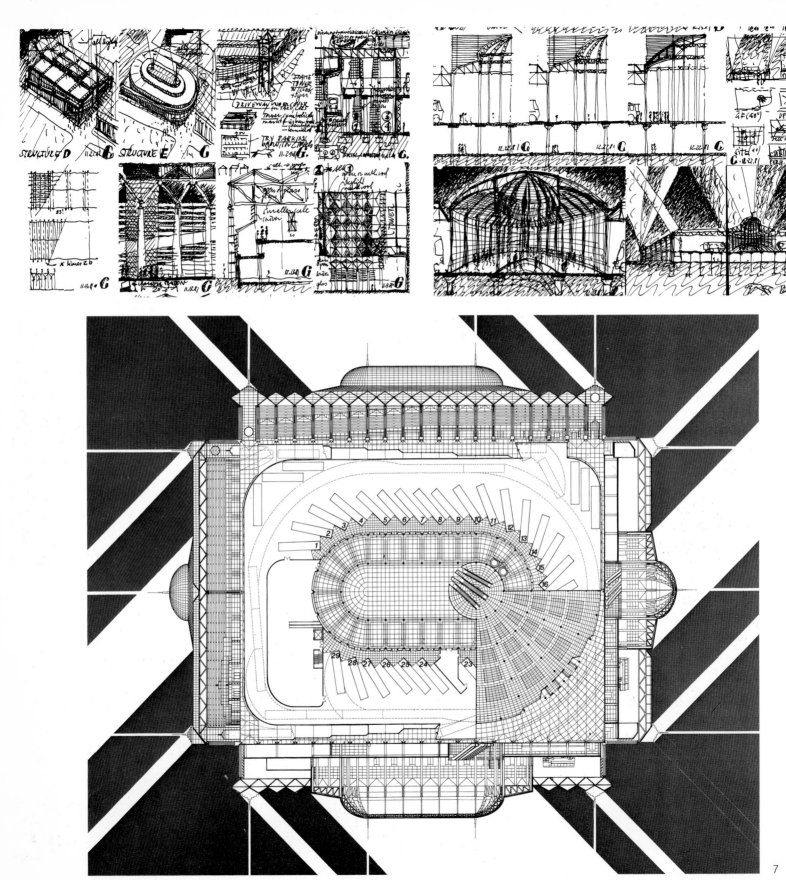

AMERICANA PLAZA

CHICAGO, IL.
Design begun 1982.

The commission is a scaled-down version of the firm's North Loop Redevelopment Plan involving a block that borders on the Chicago River. The program includes a 690-room hotel with convention facilities, an 880,000-square-foot office tower, 150,000 square feet of retail and a transit station at ground level. The 31-story office building is placed in one corner, with office floors ranging from 26,000 to 33,000 square feet and the hotel is placed diagonally across in the opposite corner. The location of the hotel takes advantage of river views. Both towers wrap around the center of the block to maintain continuous frontage towards the streets and create space for a multi-story glass-enclosed atrium with a free-standing four-story pavilion housing restaurants, ballrooms, meeting rooms and a rooftop cafe. Two levels of parking are provided below grade.

A granite arcade encircles the base and erupts into an exaggerated Palladian archway at each corner. The 75-foot-high arches are emphatic doorways that lead through retail arcades and lobbies to the atrium in the center. Above each corner an illuminated spire dramatically signals both the building and its entrances. The complex is detailed as glass-covered buildings emerging from an enclosure of horizontally-banded granite. The granite planes—intended to make a sympathetic transition to the older masonry buildings, bridge towers and riverfront promenade nearby—step back gradually and disappear revealing the glass buildings within. The glass sheathing is also revealed at each corner which is fully transparent behind the silhouettes of the gateway entrances, reinforcing its character as a "seam." The complex arrangement of towers, claddings and stepped greenhouse enclosures is intended to reduce the apparent mass of the building by expressing the many different parts while maintaining both the street lines and the project's underlying unity.

1. Atrium space
2. Wacker Drive elevation, scheme 1

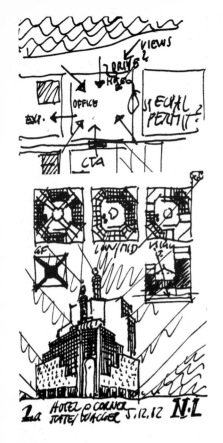

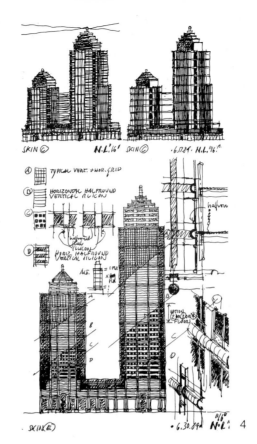

3

4

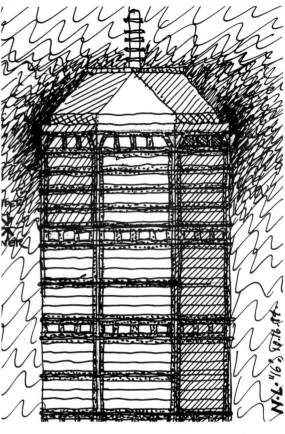

6

7

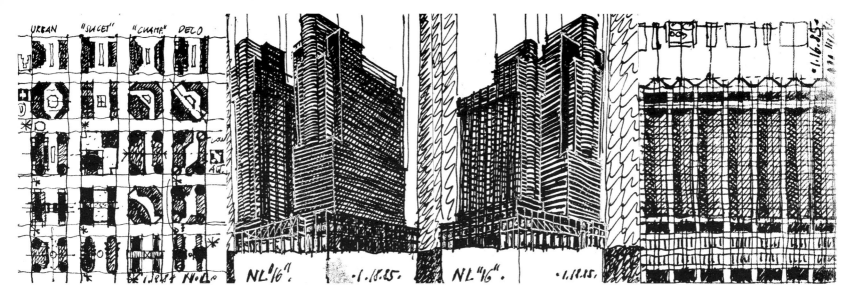

9

10

3-5. Sketches
6. Perspective of hotel/office scheme 1
7. Scheme 2 rendering
8. Scheme 3 rendering
9,11. Sketches
10. Rendering

11

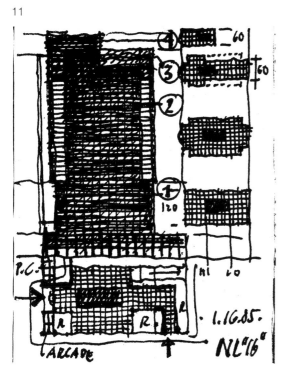

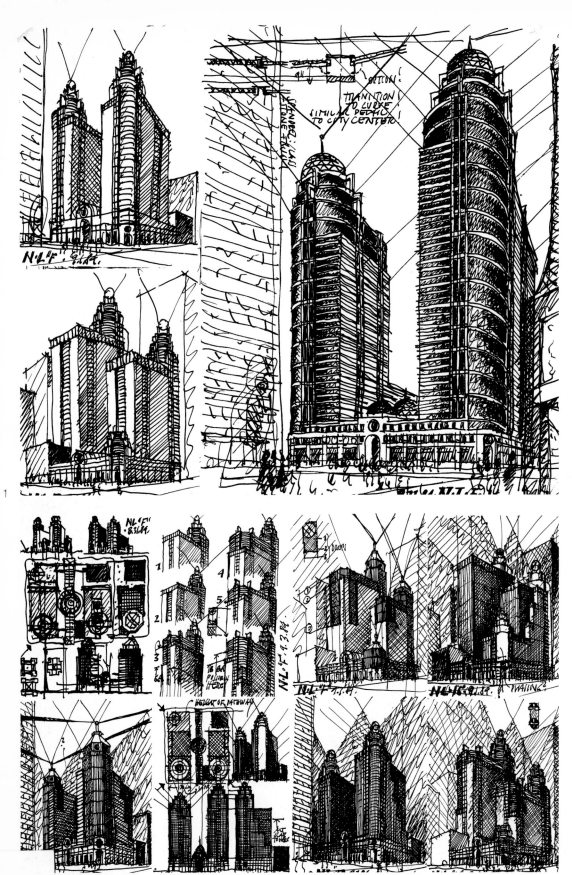

THE NORTH LOOP REDEVELOPMENT BLOCK 37

CHICAGO, ILL.
Designed in 1983

Ambitious in scale as well as intent, this project in Chicago's North Loop consists of 300,000 square feet of retail space and two office towers of 1.9 million square feet. An examination of urban form from the base treatment to the development of the tower tops, the project is organized along a 320-foot four-story pedestrian arcade which connects the office population to the west with existing retail activities to the east. The arcade and its central rotunda will be the organizing force of the retail trade, capturing a key aspect of Chicago's urban life, physically bringing together the Daley Center Plaza with Marshall Field & Co. and the great retail tradition of State Street, much in the same way that the Galleria Vittorio Emanuele in Milan provides a link between the Piazza Duomo and the La Scala Opera. Each office tower will have separate corner entries along Dearborn Street, the second-story lobbies in turn being linked directly to the arcade. The basic foot print of the towers (26,000 square feet) is designed to maximize tenant flexibility. Six tower floors in each building are reminiscent of the skyscrapers of the twenties and thirties, and offer unique opportunities for a distinguished office environment.

1

2

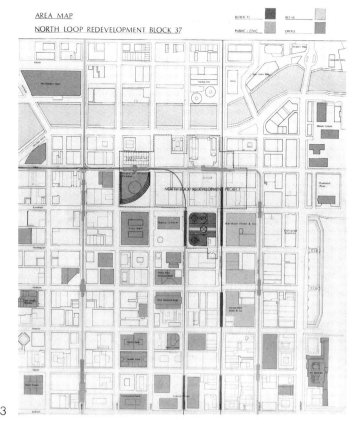

AREA MAP
NORTH LOOP REDEVELOPMENT BLOCK 37

3

4

5

6

1. 2.   Sketches
3.   Site plan
4.   Rendering
5.   Model of final scheme
6.   Scheme 2 model
Overleaf:
7.   Perspective rendering
8.   Front elevation
9.   Shopping arcade and atrium

165

7

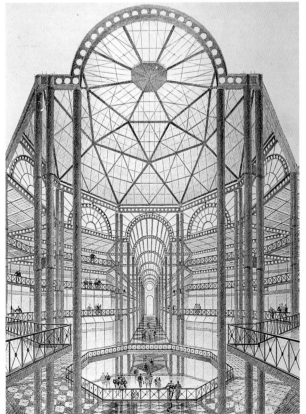

SHAND MORAHAN CORPORATE HEADQUARTERS

EVANSTON, IL.
Design begun 1982,
construction completed 1984.

The 167,000-square-foot corporate headquarters is organized as an L-shaped building that curves around the front edges of its triangular site while presenting a dramatic entrance at the corner. This arrangement allows another 150,000 square feet to be added later, an addition that would complete the only apparent symmetry. The building is narrow, 90 feet, to allow all employees to be within 45 feet of a window.

The arcade that lines the street frontages rises to double height at the corner, to emphasize that this is the entry. The wall behind is all glass to present to a giant post-and-lintel frame in front of the doorway. The exaggerated scale is preparation for the double-height lobby within.

A two-story space similar to the lobby occupies the seventh and eighth floor. It is set back and curves above the roof line to provide—from the exterior—the formal resolution of the interlocking notched patterns of the facade. Its roof is sheathed in copper, a detail picked up from a number of its older neighbors in the central area.

The street facades are composed to suggest that a sheer glass structure is emerging from a more traditional masonry one. The masonry wall is similar to a glazed curtainwall with thin-cut granite hung on an aluminum mullion system. The light and dark gray granite panels are flush and divided by bands of polished black granite which incorporate the half-round sills and lintels. The windows are recessed, glazed with gray-tinted reflective glass and banded with contrasting blue-green metal trim. The curtainwall above is sheathed in silver reflective glass with butt-glazed vertical mullions but prominent blue-green half rounds on the horizontal that correspond with the black granite banding below.

1. Plan/perspective rendering in prismacolor
2. Front detail

2

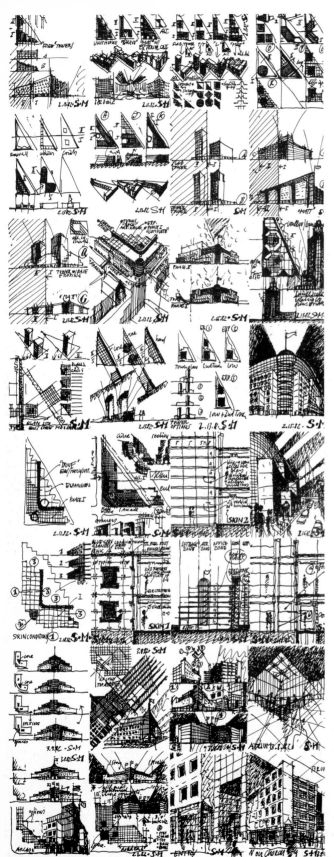

3

4

3. Sketches
4. Overall view looking west
5. View looking north with courtyard at left
6. Arcade detail
7. Overall view looking southeast
8. Courtyard

5

8

9

10

11

9. Curved corner facade
10. Entrance detail
11. Interior atrium at upper office level
12. Entrance lobby

12

13. Overall view from corner

701 FOURTH AVENUE SOUTH

MINNEAPOLIS, MN.
Design begun 1982,
construction completed 1984.

The 316,000-square-foot office tower occupies a quarter-block downtown site. Its two-story base maintains the street pattern, except at the corner where it is eroded to create a strong entrance. The two-story lobby within is flanked by retail shops and connected to neighboring buildings and a parking garage, in the Minneapolis skyway tradition.

Above the base, the 18-story octagonal office tower is composed of an inner tower with one facet squarely facing the corner wrapped by an outer ring that steps back asymmetrically from that corner. The octagonal plan allows offices facing the interior of the site to enjoy longer views, provides at least eight corner offices per floor, and permits a facade composition centered on the corner such that the two street elevations together read as a single front. Both the tower and the ring contain office space, with a range of floor sizes from 16,600 to 18,400 square feet. Tenants on floors 3, 7, 11, and 15 have access to landscaped roof terraces created by the setbacks and the 9800-square-foot penthouse has a terrace around 70 percent of its perimeter.

The articulation of the building's volume—as if it were several interconnecting volumes—is intended to reduce the bulkiness of its appearance. This goal is further pursued by varying the skin expression, contrasting a bold outer ring to a sleek core and giving special treatment to both top and bottom. The base and outer ring are sheathed in a silver blue superframe that is filled with silver reflective glass with gray mullions. At its bottom are granite pedestals and red glazed borders outlining the frame. Above the doorway is an emblematic octagon in red and blue. The frame continues at the top edge, while the glass stops short to clarify its visual

rather than structural purpose. And at the very top of the building, the setback penthouse and mechanical floor are banded in superimposed silver and red glass. Further, each horizontal bar of the superframe is edged in white spandrel glass, establishing a rhythm of horizontal stripes. This rhythm is echoed on the inner core's sheer curtainwall of blue reflective glass with blue mullions by bands of silver spandrel glass at the same intervals.

The structural system is reinforced concrete flat plate with trapezoidal bays of approximately 20 feet by 30 feet, supported on drilled caissons that bear on limestone bedrock 50 feet below grade. Approximately 45 percent of the glazing is vision glass and all the exterior glass is insulated.

Preceding page:
1. Overall view from Fourth Avenue South
2. Sketches
3. Overall view looking down on roof terraces
4. Axonometric, site plan, ground floor plan, and 15th-17th floor plans

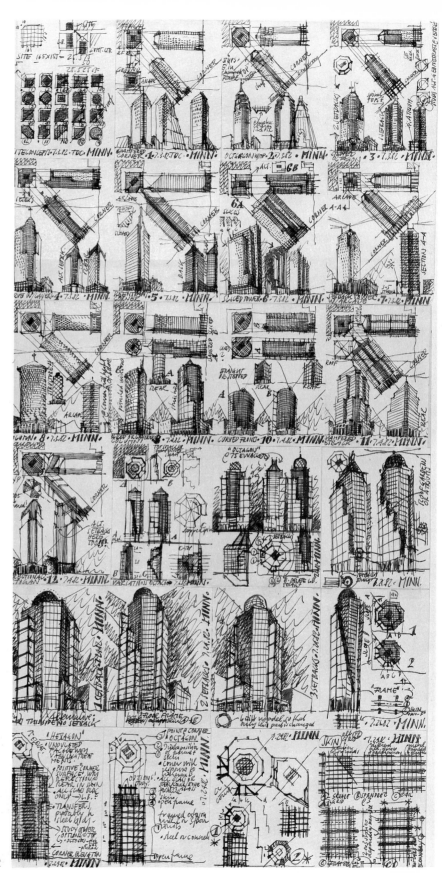

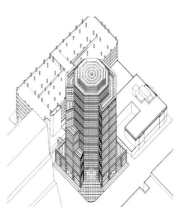

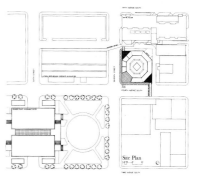

Site Plan

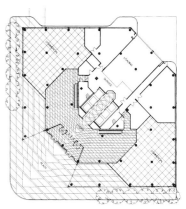

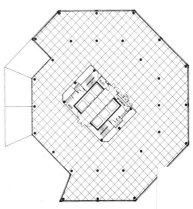

5

6

5. Overall view looking west
6. Overall view looking northeast
7. Entrance detail
8. Elevation at street level, Fourth Avenue South
9. Elevator lobby at second level
10. Entrance lobby detail
11. Entrance detail
12. Overall view of entrance facade

12

BANK OF THE SOUTHWEST TOWER

Winning Competition Entry.
HOUSTON, TX.
Design begun 1982.
In association with
Lloyd Jones Brewer Associates.

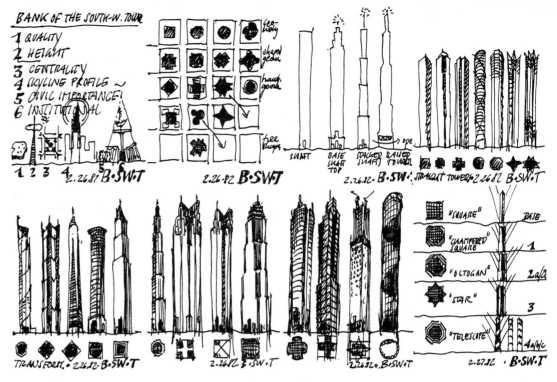

The competition program proposed the tallest building—82 stories—outside Chicago or New York, and stressed a distinct image, prominent entry, major public space and a three-dimensional exterior wall of rich, traditional surfaces. The firm won the competition with a design that makes a firm footprint on the ground, then surges upward in an obelisk form and culminates in a 130-foot spire. The tower is rotated on its full-block site so that the elevations face corners instead of streets. At each corner, one hundred-foot-high gabled porticos are placed to usher passersby into a ten-story arcade filled with shops, restaurants and art and which is connected to Houston's

underground passageway system. The formal expression of the base uses abstracted classical forms in granite to emphasize its strength and solidity.

Above, the slimmer office tower sets back gradually, forming five distinguishable sections within the overall tapering form. At top, the obelisk culminates not in the expected pyramid but in an elaborately faceted form without direct historic precedent. The elevations are sheathed in a pattern of materials with gabled sections in aluminum and reflective glass, the massive piers in glass and two types of granite, and the chamfered corners in glass set flush with silicone joints.

An innovative structural system, based on internal bracing and combining concrete and steel systems, was developed by consulting engineer William Le Messurier for the two million-square-foot building. It involves eight reinforced concrete columns, set 80 feet apart on either side of the chamfered corners, buttressed by four vertical steel trusses, two in each direction. The columns are 10 by 20 feet thick at the base, narrowing to 5 by 5 feet at the top. Among the advantages of this system are 80-foot spans within the building and an exterior free from the close-set columns or cross-bracing that the other cost-efficient systems require.

1. Sketches
2. Seven original schemes
3. Sketches
Overleaf:
4. Sketches
5. Overall view of model
6. Split section/elevation rendering
7. Contextual view
8. Base rendering

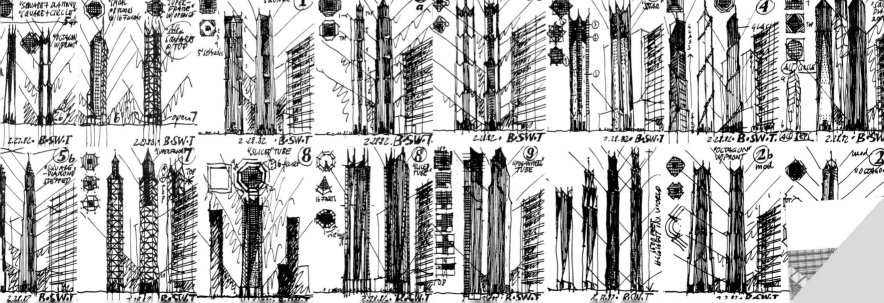

4

5

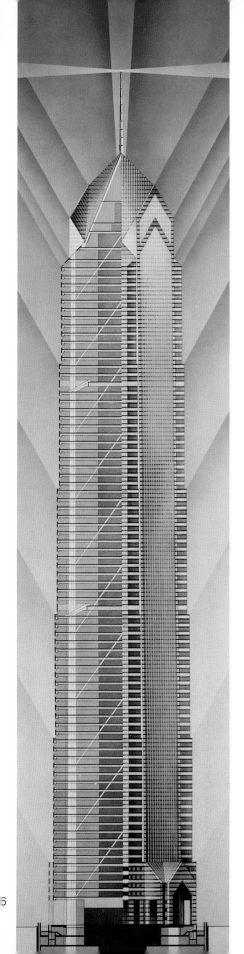

6

7

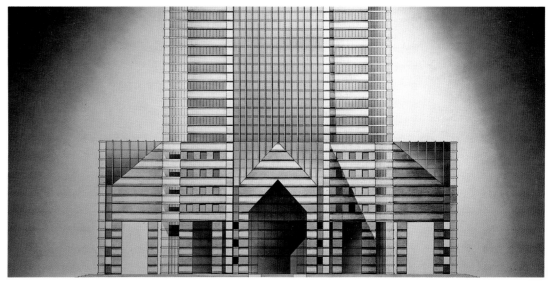

8

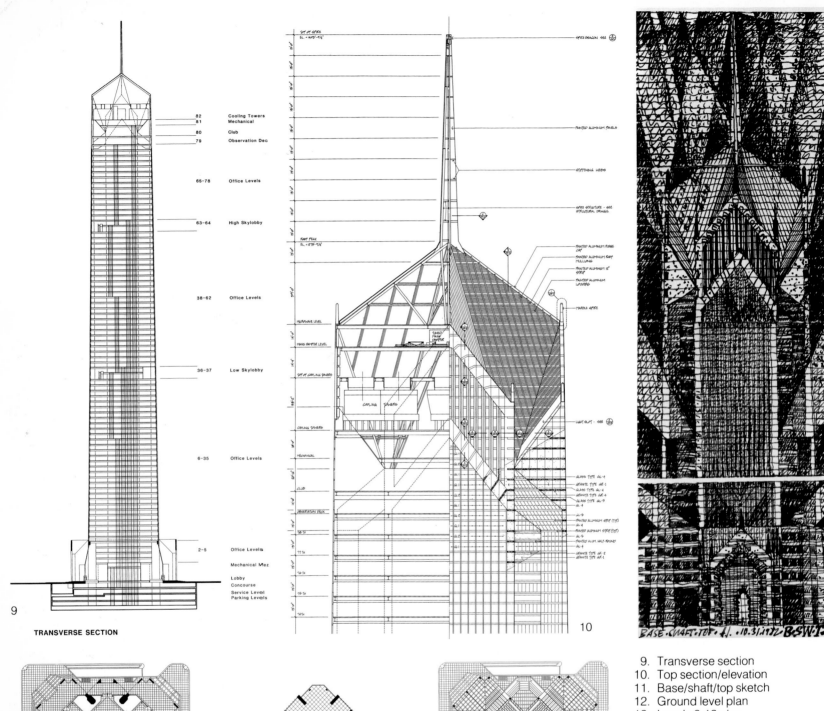

9

TRANSVERSE SECTION

82	Cooling Towers
81	Mechanical
80	Club
79	Observation Dec
65–78	Office Levels
63–64	High Skylobby
38–62	Office Levels
36–37	Low Skylobby
6–35	Office Levels
2–5	Office Levels
	Mechanical Mez
	Lobby
	Concourse
	Service Level
	Parking Levels

10

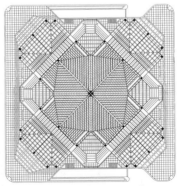

BASE · SHAFT · TOP · # · 10.31.1972 · BSWT

9. Transverse section
10. Top section/elevation
11. Base/shaft/top sketch
12. Ground level plan
13. Levels 6-12 plan
14. Roof plan

12

13

14

182

362 WEST STREET

DURBAN, WEST AFRICA.
Design begun 1982,
completion estimated 1985.
In association with
Stauch Vorster and Partners.

1

1. West Street elevation
2. Aerial view
3. Overall view
4. Cityscape

The firm was asked for something as "exciting" as 11 Diagonal Street by the developers that had commissioned that building in Johannesburg the year before. The firm responded by adapting its Humana competition entry. The 24-story office tower consists of an inner and outer octagon with the outer octagon rising around the inner one in a helical pattern. The arrangement provides accessible landscaped roof terraces off each floor, that look out over the Bay and the Indian Ocean as well as the subtropical port city. The spire at the top houses microwave and communication equipment, a detail that was intended to complement what the firm felt was already science fiction imagery. Shopfronts are provided along the sidewalks in a retail arcade at mid-block and the lobby.

Each element is expressed in distinguishable architectural terms. The outer octagon has a strong supergrid that is defined by bundled corner columns and triangular sections of blue and silver glass within which is a smaller grid of white mullions at the floor-to-floor scale. In contrast, the inner octagon is sheathed in a flush silver skin that ties into the rhythms of the outer shell with horizontal bands at floor levels. The retail arcades unfold in a system of glazed canopies that are intended to punctuate the distinctness of individual shops and provide the variety expected at street level.

The structural system of the tower is reinforced concrete with concrete shear walls at the core to provide lateral stiffness and more openness at ground level. The shops are conventionally framed in steel while the associated arcades and canopies are elaborately detailed with shop-fabricated steel frames and bundled columns to recall the wrought ironwork of nineteenth century arcades.

5

190

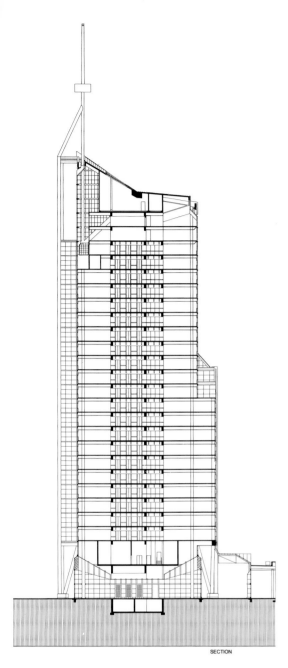

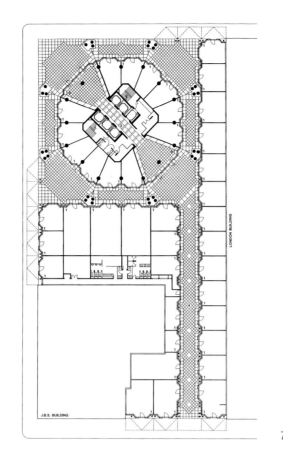

SECTION

7

8

5. Spiral top
6. Section
7. Ground floor plan
8. Floor plans
9. Vertical circulation serving upper floors
   Overleaf:
10. Interior arcade
11. Aerial view
12. Connecting arcade entrance on
    other side of block
13. Storefront detail, arcade
14. Corner view
15. View of arcade

6

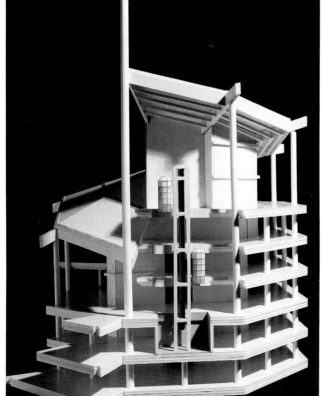

9

10

11

12

13

14

15

CODEX CORPORATION HEADQUARTERS

Competition Entry.
MANSFIELD, MA.
Designed in 1982.

The firm's entry for a new office headquarters that would be consonant with the preservation of its special site, Maresfield Farm, is a two-story building organized radially around a landscaped courtyard, and filled with natural light via skylights and clerestories. A special section housing the conference and employee dining facilities is located on the other side of the driveway from the office building but is connected by a central spine. Atria branch out from the spine to allow daylight to filter down to ground level spaces.

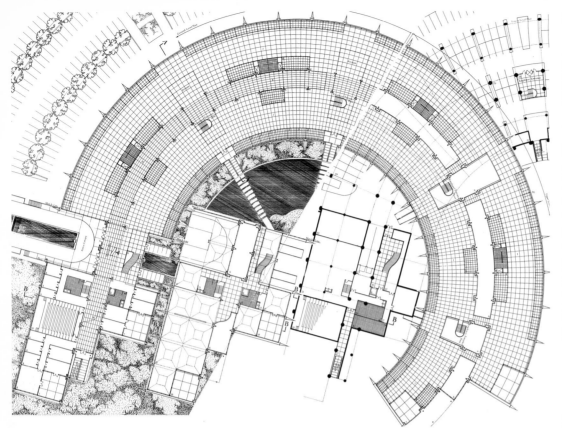

1

1. Section
2. Axonometric
3. West elevation
4. Aerial view

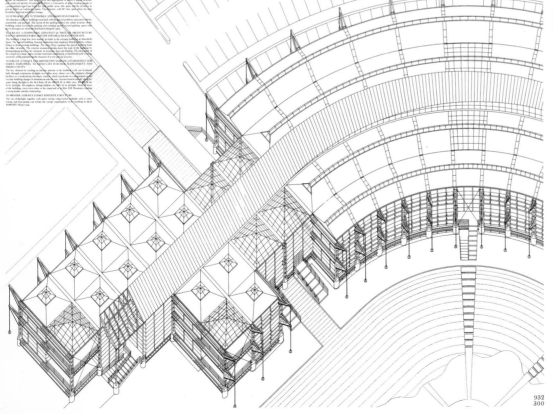

2

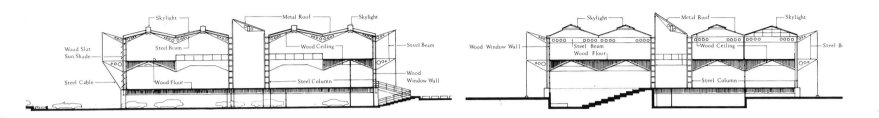

3

4

197

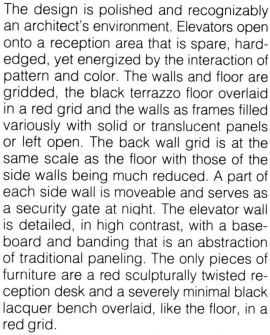

MURPHY/JAHN OFFICES

CHICAGO, IL.
Design begun 1982,
construction completed 1982.

The design is polished and recognizably an architect's environment. Elevators open onto a reception area that is spare, hard-edged, yet energized by the interaction of pattern and color. The walls and floor are gridded, the black terrazzo floor overlaid in a red grid and the walls as frames filled variously with solid or translucent panels or left open. The back wall grid is at the same scale as the floor with those of the side walls being much reduced. A part of each side wall is moveable and serves as a security gate at night. The elevator wall is detailed, in high contrast, with a base-board and banding that is an abstraction of traditional paneling. The only pieces of furniture are a red sculpturally twisted reception desk and a severely minimal black lacquer bench overlaid, like the floor, in a red grid.

A stair, composed of structural trusses painted red and visible from the lobby, hints that the firm occupies more than this floor. The space, in fact, includes two partial floors in addition to the main level, a total of 27,000 square feet. The reception area leads to either the open drafting rooms which occupy the spaces on three sides of the central core or a linear suite of offices on the fourth. Grids reappear throughout. The larger grid appears in free-standing partitions with infills of solid, translucent and transparent panels in stepped

1. View towards executive office
2. Reception
3. Executive conference area
4. Executive secretaries' desks
5. Main circulation corridor

patterns. The translucent and transparent glass are further quartered by faux mullions silkscreened in red. Smaller grids are laminated onto window walls and underscore the older building's large, arched windows. Core walls continue as abstractions of traditionally panelled walls with banding and reveals.

The color palette juxtaposes red detailing and accessories against four shades of blue-gray. The lightest tone is used on walls and ceilings. The other three are used for the gridded frames in a graduated hierarchy; the denser the grid, the darker the color. Furnishings were mainly recycled from the firm's previous office space, although new work stations were purchased for studio areas. Existing drawing and correspondence files were electrostatically refinished in the lightest blue-gray and either built into the walls or left freestanding to serve as pedestals for study models. Teak, walnut and oak tables were ebonized. The lighting is predominantly soft, diffused and indirect with wall washers in reception and office areas and track lighting above corridors.

6. Public and private corridors
7. Executive office
8. Drafting area
9. Executive office
10. Floor plan

6

7

9

10

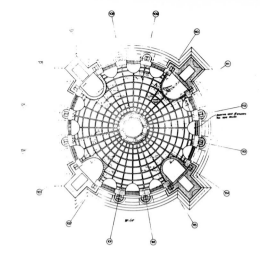

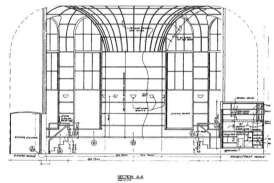

SECTION A-A

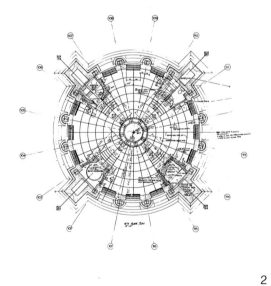

2

1. Cupola ceiling
2. Reflected ceiling plan, section, and floor plan
3. Cupola space with bird cage elevator entry
4. Cupola, presentation space

1

CUPOLA

35 EAST WACKER DRIVE
CHICAGO, ILL.
Designed in 1983

The original 1,800-square-foot, 27-foot-high space was stripped to the bone, and the entity of the dome re-created for this Murphy/Jahn client presentation/conference area. Four service modules were placed around two axes of symmetry, sub-dividing the circle into four quadrants around the centrally located smokestack which unfortunately had to remain in the middle of the space. The floor was raised 36 inches to allow for a better view over an unusually high parapet. Floors and walls were articulated with bands and grids, in the manner of the Murphy/Jahn office on the third floor of the same building. Lighting is hidden behind slanted cornices at service modules, uplighting the highly patterned ceiling to reflect the floor below. Additional lighting is provided by wall sconces. Furnishings (yet to be executed) are subordinated to the project presentation/conference function with four square tables/model pedestals in each of the quadrants. An elaborate, round elevator, reminiscent of French cage-type elevators rises for the last five floors terminating at the cupula. Respect for the inherent features of this early twenties structure was combined and enriched by a contemporary wall articulative.

4

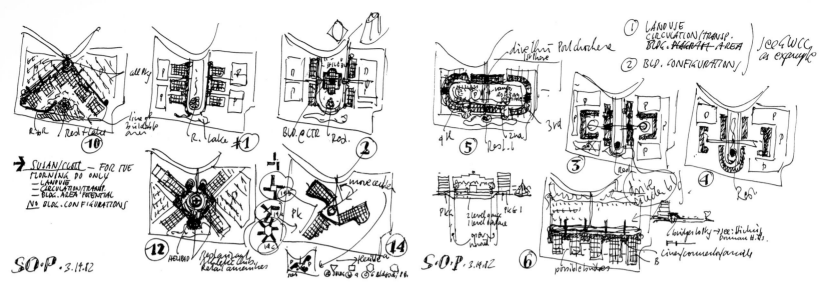

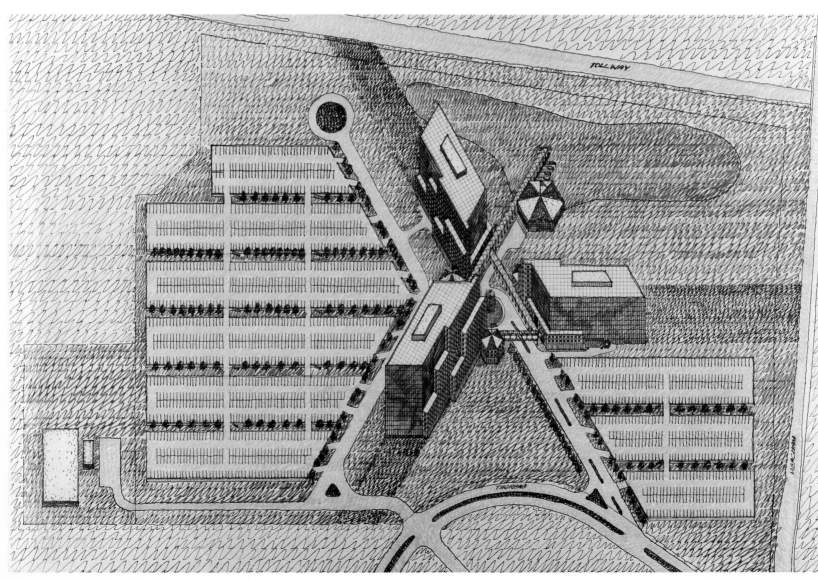

THE QUORUM/ WOODFIELD

SCHAUMBURG, IL.
Designed in 1982.

The 46-acre office park is planned to provide one million square feet in three stages, as part of a larger mixed-use development that includes housing, a hotel and neighborhood shops and restaurants. Three office buildings are arranged around a central courtyard, which is encircled by a translucent arcade to provide bad weather connections from building to building and to parking. There is also a 7000-square-foot conference center pavilion at the edge of the site's retention pond, connected to the other buildings by an extended leg of the arcade.

Each building has a different configuration but the elements are consistent: a glass-skinned rhomboid with seemingly random layers clad in masonry. This contrast is emphasized by a pinwheel organization which juxtaposes the glass side of one building with the stone side of another. In addition, the stone varies in color from building to building.

1. Sketches
2. Axonometric site plan
3. Sketches
4. Elevation rendering
5. Model view looking southwest
6. View of connecting arcade

3

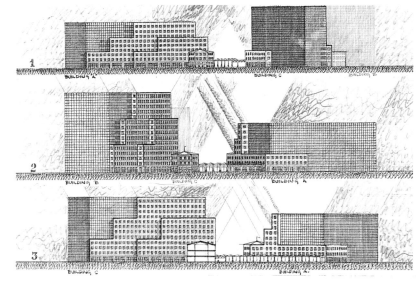

4

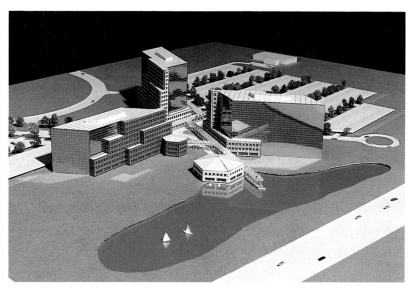

5

6

PARK AVENUE TOWER

NEW YORK, NY.
Design begun 1983,
completion estimated 1986.

The 36-story office tower occupies a through-block location in midtown Manhattan. The first scheme was a twin-topped tower presenting a curved and faceted facade to each street frontage. But the design that is being built is obelisk-shaped. Tapering sides and corners of glass and granite with stepped-back glass infill culminate in a characteristic pyramid, the very tip of which is purely symbolic.

The tower contains 480,000 square feet of office rental space on 35 floors with varied floor areas. The primary entrance is recessed behind a small granite and marble forecourt flanked by arcades. Commercial space buttresses the tower lobby at ground level and two subgrade levels provide parking and more rental area. The exterior materials include gray reflective glass with projecting tubular vertical mullions and both flame-cut and polished angola black granite with projecting tubular horizontal mullions.

1   2   3   4

Murphy Jahn   Murphy Jahn   Murphy Jahn   Murphy Jahn

7

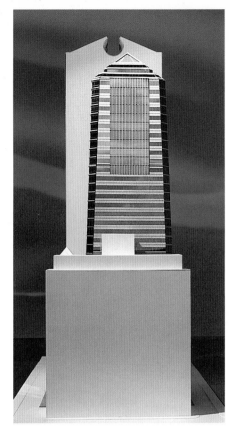

13

14

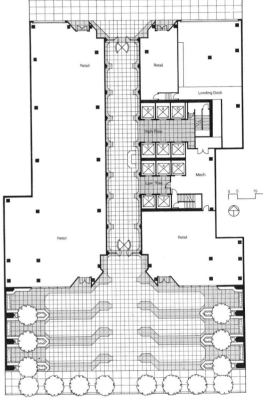

15

13. Sketches
14. Entrance corridor
15. Floor plans

425 LEXINGTON AVENUE

NEW YORK, N.Y.
Design begun 1983.

The speculative office tower is located in midtown Manhattan, across the street from the landmark Chrysler Building. The design is a deliberate variation on the tower-as-architectural-column proposals to the 1922 Chicago Tribune Competition by Adolf Loos and others. The setback shaft with a wider top and base meshes with midtown's new zoning requirements and takes advantage of the available bonuses while providing a range of floor sizes. The 28 office rental floors range in size from 26,900 to 16,900 square feet—552,000 square feet altogether—with commercial space at ground level. The chamfered plan allows a variety of corner offices and affords longer views. A special penthouse floor offers 23-foot ceilings and two below-grade levels provide parking and more rental space. The main entrance is signaled by a deep, multi-story recess that echoes the silhouette of the whole building and a second entrance is reached through a small landscaped plaza at mid-block, on the other side of the building. Both entrances lead into 20-foot-high marble lobbies with coffered, luminous ceilings, and between the two lobbies runs a shop-lined galleria.

The chamfered, terraced, flared and straight surfaces of the tower are sheathed in a palette of reflective and textured glass, half round and triangular mullions, and veneers of granite, marble and limestone. The patterns are intended to ameliorate some of the proportions, present the scale of the building in accessible terms and knit the various elements together. Dark green granite, green marble and buff-colored limestone line the walls at street level to introduce a higher quality of finish where people come in closest contact with the building.

The structural system is moment connected steel frame supporting a 5½-inch concrete slab on cellular metal decking. A variety of rectangular bay sizes, approximately 30 feet by 40 feet, provide column-free lease spans on a typical tower floor. Loads from columns located along the perimeter setbacks of the base are transferred to the floor below and chamfered corners are cantilevered.

1. Model of final scheme
2-5. Alternative schemes

1

2

3

4

5

6

A_{M1}   7

B_{M9}   8

C_{M1}   9

D_{M2}   1

E_{M2}   11

13

12

213

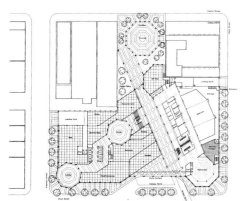

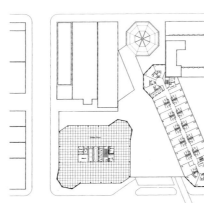

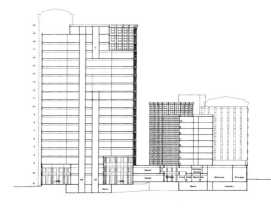

3

4

5

225

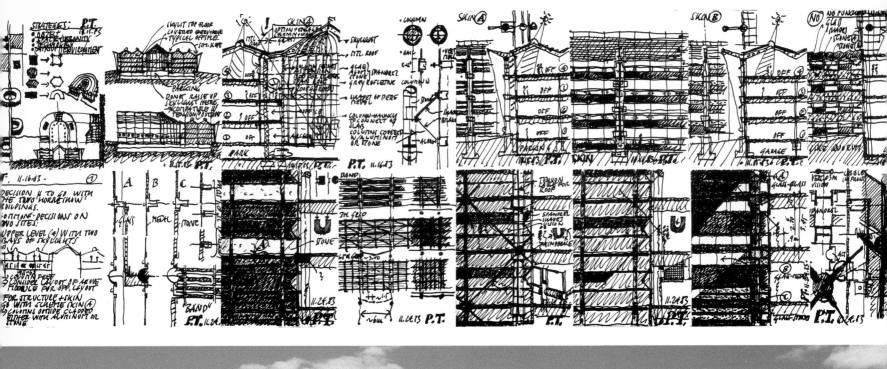

PARKTOWN STANDS
102, 103, 85, 879

JOHANNESBURG, SOUTH AFRICA
Design begun 1983;
completion estimated 1986.
In association with
John Kemp & Associates.

Parktown Stands 102, 103, 85, and 879 are components of a design plan for a suburban office park of 18-meter-wide U-shaped buildings that curve around a covered plaza, which in turn acts as the building library. The plan of each building is organized as two buildings, each with its own separate core and lobby, offering maximum flexibility for tenant layouts as well as a more positive identity for larger tenants. A two-story-high pedestrian passage bisects each building, providing a connection between the formal garden of the covered plaza with the more natural landscape of the rest of the site. Silver textured glass and perforated-metal sunshades add high-tech color, while the green and rust color of the skin recalls the lush vegetation of the surrounding area and the red color of the soil. Daylighting plays an important role in the concept of the skin and form. Clear glass is used in concert with perforated sunshades on the north and east facades to control the amount of sunlight in the office areas. The third floor has the additional feature of two continuous skylights that in effect provide a floor that is 90 percent lit by daylight.

1. Sketches
2. The covered plaza
3-5. Views of the model

3

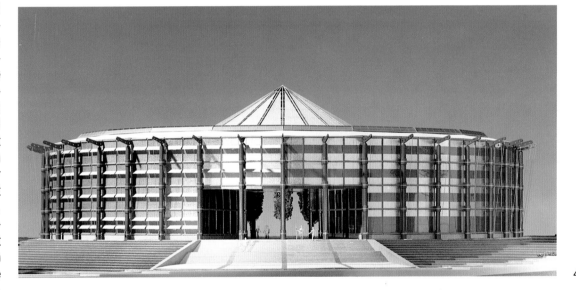

4

5

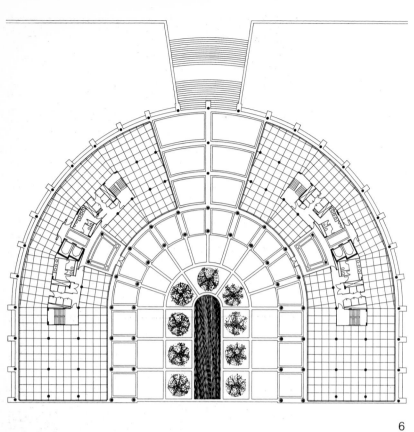

6

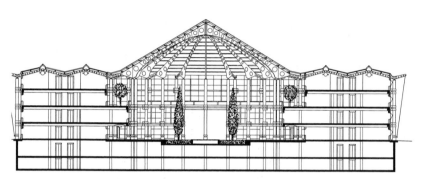

7

8

9

10

1

229

TWO ENERGY CENTER

Naperville, Ill.
Construction:

Two Energy Center, a ten-story, 232,000-square-foot speculative office development, consists of two buildings linked by an enclosed atrium, raised on a landscaped podium base. The buildings' cubic forms are set at a 45-degree angle on the axis of the platform area. The curvilinear atrium, suspended from opposing faces of the buildings, becomes an independent geometry—polygonal in plan and undulating in elevation. The facade consists of an inner and outer curtain wall, offset 15 feet by a diagonal skylight, the offset in plan allowing for two ample floors of rental space at the base with a progressive reduction in depth and area from floors three through ten. In elevation the outer wall establishes a major framework in aluminum projected beyond a flush wall of granite panels punctuated by window openings, with half-round aluminum moldings at head and sill. The interior wall is a flush plane of silicone-glazed, tinted and reflective glass panels with continuous horizontal half-round moldings modulating the surface. Facade and plan configurations within a simple cube and gridwork geometry provide a detailed visual image within this suburban office/research park.

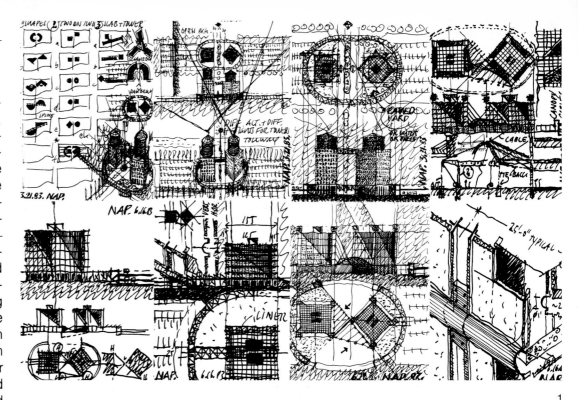

1

1. Sketches
2. Perspective rendering

230

FRANKFURT CONVENTION CENTER

Competition Entry.
FRANKFURT AM MAIN, GERMANY
Designed in 1984.

The competition called for a new exhibition hall, a speculative office tower, and a network of entries and connections to be added to buildings already on the site, including a 1900 *Festhalle* by Friedrich von Thiersch and the more recent *Kongresshalle*. The firm's entry considers three alternate tower designs, each raised above the ground to form a grand gateway to the complex, on axis with the turn-of-the-century *Festhalle*. Each tower consists of an outer shape sheathed in stone and glass or superstructure from which an inner glass form emerges. Tops and bases are distinct from the main shafts of the towers. Tower One is the most directly influenced by art deco architectural design and is a varia-

tion on proposals the firm has made in New York and Philadelphia. Structurally, it relies on a diagonally-framed steel skeleton to carry both gravity and wind loads to the four corner supports. Tower Two is an octagon with a load-bearing core, double columns around the perimeter and secondary columns on the interior. It is also a more refined version of one of the tower designs for Philadelphia. Tower Three is, in principle, similar to a sailboat mast with a compression core and prestressed tension members around the perimeter.

Surrounding the tower is a semicircular entry building connected to a series of arcades that provide clear-cut circulation between the buildings and a distinct edge against the street. Both the arcades and entry building are barrel-vaulted with metal panel infill interrupted by strips of glass block to permit sunlight to enter. The three-story exhibition hall has a space frame roof with a similar mix of opaque and glass infill for natural illumination.

1. Northeast elevation
2. Section
3. Floor plans
   Overleaf:
4. Model photo

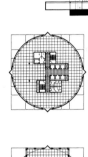

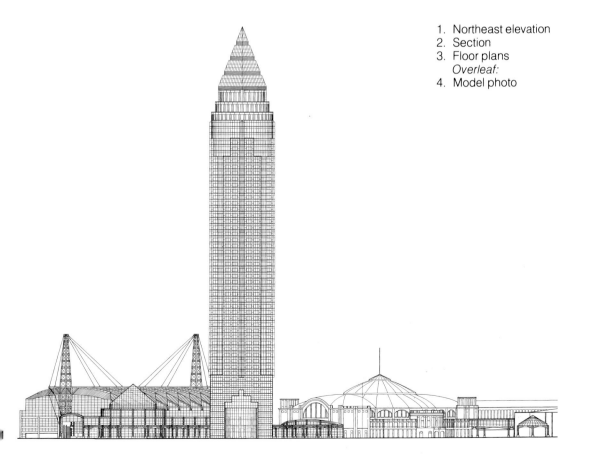

3

SAN DIEGO CONVENTION CENTER

Competition Entry.
SAN DIEGO, CA.
Designed in 1984.
Associate architects:
Martinez/Wong Associates

Unlike the hermetically sealed box of the typical post-war convention center, the firm's entry to this limited competition recreates the exuberance of early Modern work. The design combines imagery suggested by its waterside location—lighthouses, masts with rigging, decks, bridges, cranes —with forms reminiscent of one of San Diego's most distinguished landmarks, the Coronado Hotel. The elements within the project are anatomically distinguished with circulation and structure pulled out and exploited for their full decorative value. Primary structural elements, including the dramatic steel cable system, are painted bright red with secondary members of both curtainwall and metal wall system painted green. Circulation is celebrated in a vaulted glass promenade that doubles as lobby area for the meeting rooms, and in two finial-shaped greenhouses at either end within which spiraling pedestrian ramps provide vertical circulation that is as theatrical from the outside as it is visually accessible from within. All circulation areas enjoy spectacular views of the city or the water and the public terraces facing the water can be entered from both inside and from the boardwalk below.

The 690,000-square-foot building includes 250,000 square feet of exhibition space and 100,000 square feet of meeting rooms on top of a 633,650-square-foot parking structure. The substructure is reinforced concrete; the superstructure is supported by a cable system allowing 240-foot clear spans in the exhibition hall. The roof uses a rolled steel overhead truss framing system in a sawtooth configuration. Seismic resistance is provided by shear walls and lateral steel bracing in two directions.

Materials emphasize the differences between the various parts of the building. The circulation areas are wrapped in a glass curtainwall that combines translucent, opaque and transparent panels. The exhibition and meeting spaces are sheathed in a metal panel system with portal windows and covered with preformed metal roofing. Public corridors and lobbies are paved in terrazzo while the exhibition area is floored in sealed concrete and the meeting rooms are carpeted.

1. Harbor Drive perspective rendering
2. Section/perspective
3. Overall view of model

1

2

3

THE ESPLANADE

HOUSTON, TEX.
Designed in 1984

The site development concept for the Esplanade proposes an alternative to the characteristic image of the suburban office environment: individual object buildings dispersed in an open landscape and circuitously woven together by roadways and automobiles. A more urban streetscape of wide boulevards and building facades conforming to a uniform facade line are among the design principles ordering the master plan, the first phase of which is a crescent-shaped quadrant within the Esplanade's major planning feature, a circular, spatial focus at the scale of England's Royal Crescent. The building's curved facade forms a natural architectural gesture around a curved reflecting pool. The building will contain 690,000 gross square feet of space in twenty-eight rental office floors above one level of ground-floor retail space. The crescent ends are sliced to create appropriately frontal facades. Twin octagon pavilions engage the crescent at these two facades, which, when paired with formally similar crescents, will function as gateway towers to the site's major and minor axes. A single three- story setback at the top of the crescent, emerging a a pure omni-directional tower, mediates the transition between the curving facades and the two octagonal pavilions.

1. Sketches
2. Model photo

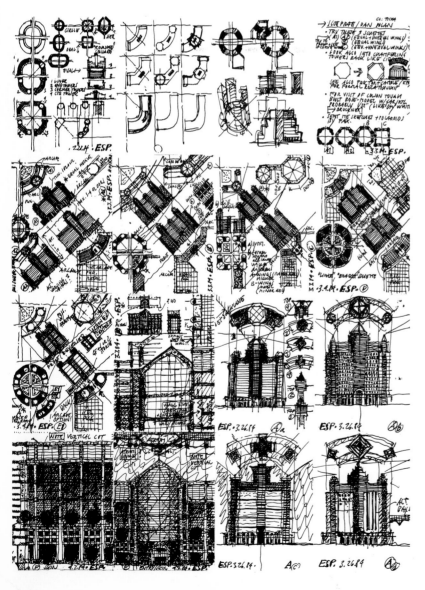

242

750 LEXINGTON

NEW YORK, N.Y.
Designed in 1984

750 Lexington will be a 30-story office tower with two floors below grade, providing a total of 375,000 gross square feet of space. The ground floor along Lexington Avenue extends beyond the outline of the tower to reinforce streetwall continuity and retail exposure. To reduce pedestrian congestion, the ground floor of the building will be surrounded by a large plaza. The basic concept of the tower design is the interlocking of two geometric volumes: a pristine cylinder wrapped by an outer volume, which changes from a rectangle to a polygon, the cylinder emerging from this form at the top as a giant bay window. The contextual aspects of the outer building are reinforced through its facade treatment of bays, in contrast to the glass skin of the cylinder. Horizontal stone spandrels at multiple numbers of floors provide continuity between outer and inner buildings. Curved, projected bays activate the retail base as a formal, conceptual link to the cylindrical form. The structural system affords large column spacing, providing increased flexibility for tenant development. The exterior curtain wall will extend from 12 inches above the floor to the 9-foot ceiling, providing unique floor-to-ceiling glass.

1

2

1. Model photo
2. Elevation/plan rendering

BROADWAY & 52ND STREET

NEW YORK, N.Y.
Designed in 1985

The three-part massing of this corner building, which will house a theater and offices, is intended to emphasize its relationship to the site and its theater and office uses. The building's entry at the corner of 52nd Street and Broadway is designed to give the office tower its own identity without distracting from that of the theater, the entrance canopy and the theater marquee being ornamental elements on the street of equal importance. The enclosure is designed to emphasize the three-part massing. The streetwall is given a single-floor reading with stone banding at every floor. The theater setbacks are given a two-story reading, while the curved office portion with its four-story banding is further emphasized by the use of vertical mullions projecting from the building plane. The stone base ties the building's parts together, while the top typifies the ambience of Broadway and Times Square with its rotating message center and spire. The building is constructed of structural steel utilizing a series of transfers expressed at the 53rd Street setbacks in order to span the theater, thereby minimizing impact on its operations.

1. Perspective rendering

1

244

TEN COLUMBUS CIRCLE

NEW YORK, N.Y.
Designed in 1985

Ten Columbus Circle will be a multiuse complex of office, hotel, and residential spaces totaling approximately 2.64 million square feet of new construction. The complex is composed of the 85-foot-high base structure, which will reinforce the Columbus Circle geometry and establish the inner plaza; and the tower structure, which at a height of 1,275 feet will be an easily recognizable image on the Manhattan skyline. The base structure is treated as a highly ornamented building in itself, utilizing stone and glass as infill material within a structural expression on a scale smaller than that of the tower. The inner plaza is meant to continue the logical progression from the open space of Central Park through the orientation point of the Circle. The tower is a segmented hollow octagonal tube raised 100 feet above grade. A 230-foot-high slot is provided to reinforce the 59th Street view corridor that was previously vacated at this site. The first fifteen floors will provide approximately 1,156,675 square feet of office space. Above the setback skylobby level rise hotel and residential floors which terrace up in a spiraling configuration, providing commanding views of Central Park and the Hudson River.

1. Perspective rendering

TELEVISION CITY™

NEW YORK, N.Y.
Designed in 1985

Television City™ is a mixed-use waterfront development of 19.5 million square feet of commercial, residential, and retail space that will include both the world's most advanced television and motion-picture production complex and the world's tallest building, a mixed-use 150-story tower. The now vacant 100-acre site, formerly the Penn Central Railroad yards, is the largest undeveloped tract on Manhattan's West Side, stretching along the Hudson River from West 59th Street in the south to West 72nd Street in the north. Nearly 8,000 units of residential space for some 20,000 tenants are planned together with 1.8 million square feet of retail space and 9,600 parking spaces. The project includes 3.6 million square feet of television and motion-picture studios, and technical and office space. The waterfront and piers are to be renovated to incorporate a 13-block waterfront promenade in addition to some forty acres of parkland and open spaces.

1. Model, view from the Hudson River
2. Site plan
3. Elevation/plan rendering

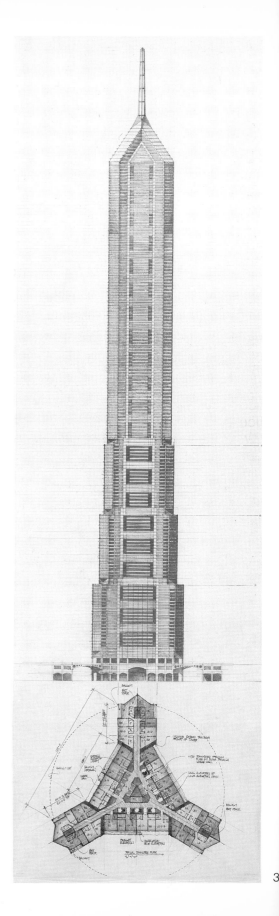

1

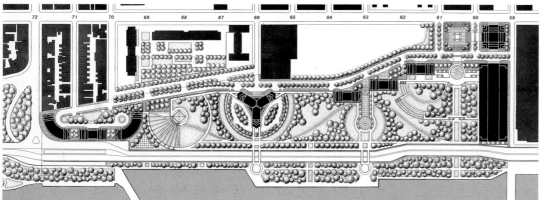
3

2

MONARCH PLAZA II

ATLANTA, GA.
Designed in 1985

Monarch Plaza II is the third phase of the existing Monarch Plaza development which currently consists of a 16-story office building, the Ritz Carlton Hotel, and a parking deck accommodating 1,500 cars situated on a 12¾-acre site in Atlanta's Buckhead district. The Monarch Plaza II project consists of a 27-story office tower built atop a new 1,900-car parking deck. The tower serves as a backdrop for a new motor court and entry arcade built on top of the existing parking structure. The radial pedestrian arcade fronts new retail space surrounding the motor court. The pedestrian arcade extends from the retail and motor-court plaza down between the existing hotel and office building to define the office tower's address and identity. The office building itself is an omnidirectional tower clad in reflective, textured, and opaque glass, accented by vertical stone pieces. The tower terminates in a series of terne-coated stainless-steel cross vaults. The tower lobby, finished in stone, is integrated into the pedestrian interior arcade which connects the office building to the retail area, other existing building functions, and the new entry arcade.

1. East elevation rendering
2. Ground/site plan
3. Overall model view

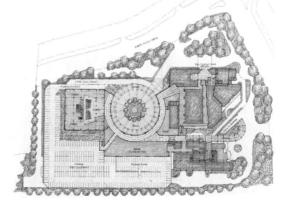

THE OAKBROOK TERRACE TOWER

CHICAGO, ILL.
Designed in 1985

The Oakbrook Terrace Tower will provide 663,000 square feet of office space in a 29-story tower. Its clear identity as architectural object in concert with a ceremonial approach and lobby atria reinforces the elegance and monumentality of the design. The tower is an octagon in plan with emphasis on the orthogonal planes, thus allowing for its unique vertical expression. The four diagonal faces employ a horizontal expression that, when played against the vertical, provides for a high level of visual interest. This play of horizontal and vertical becomes the generator of the tower's signature space at the top of the building, which will provide a unique opportunity for the tenant who requires a distinct identity. Penetrations in the ground floor will provide for visual continuity with the lower-level lobby. Current plans envision the use of the existing Dispensed Castle basements as tenant storage.

1. Elevation rendering
2. Office terrace

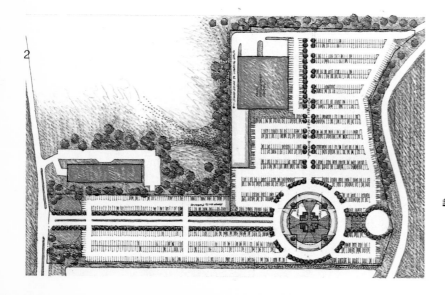

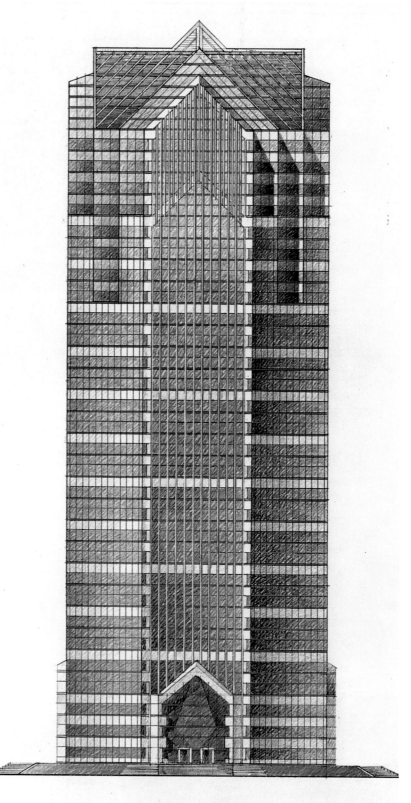

The Oakbrook Terrace Tower
Murphy/Jahn

BIOGRAPHY

1940   Born, January 4, Nürnberg, Germany

1965   Graduated from Technische Hochschule, Munich, Germany

1965–66   Worked with P. C. von Seidlein, Munich, Germany

1966–67   Graduate studies, Illinois Institute of Technology, with Myron Goldsmith and Fazlur Kahn

1970   Married to Deborah Lampe

1978   Birth of first child, Evan

1967–73   Assistant to Gene Summers at C. F. Murphy Associates

1973   Executive Vice President and Director of Planning and Design at C. F. Murphy Associates

1975   Corporate member of American Institute of Architects

1975   Registered Architect NCARB; state registrations in Illinois, California, Colorado, Florida, Indiana, Minnesota, New York, Texas, and Virginia

1977   Selected for inclusion in 40th edition *Who's Who in America*

1980   Honorary Degree Doctor of Fine Arts, St. Mary's College, Notre Dame, Indiana

1980   Selected for inclusion in 5th edition *Who's Who in Technology Today*

1981   Principal, Murphy/Jahn

1982   President, Murphy/Jahn

1983   President and CEO, Murphy/Jahn

Spring 1981   University of Illinois Circle Campus, Chicago, Illinois, Design Studio

Fall 1981   Harvard University, Elliot Noyes Professor of Architectural Design

Winter/Spring 1983   Yale University, Davenport Visiting Professor of Architectural Design

COMPLETED BUILDINGS

1974   Kemper Arena, Kansas City, Missouri

1975   Auraria Library, Denver, Colorado

1976   Fourth District Courts Building, Maywood, Illinois

1976   John Marshall Courts Building, Richmond, Virginia

1976   H. Roe Bartle Exhibition Hall, Kansas City, Missouri

1977   Michigan City Library, Michigan City, Indiana

1977   St. Mary's Athletic Facility, South Bend, Indiana

1977   Monroe Garage, Chicago, Illinois

1977   Springfield Garage, Springfield, Illinois

1978   Glenbrook Professional Building, Northbrook, Illinois

1978   La Lumiere Gymnasium, La Porte, Indiana

1978   Rust-Oleum Corporate Headquarters, Vernon Hills, Illinois

1979   Prairie Capital Convention Center, Parking Garage, Springfield, Illinois

1979   W. W. Grainger Corporate Headquarters, Skokie, Illinois

1980   Xerox Centre, Chicago, Illinois

1981   De La Garza Career Center, East Chicago, Indiana

1981   Oak Brook Post Office, Oak Brook, Illinois

1981   Commonwealth Edison District Headquarters, Downers Grove, Illinois

1981   Area 2 Police Headquarters, Chicago, Illinois

1982   Argonne Program Support Facility, Argonne, Illinois

1982   First Source Center, South Bend, Indiana

1982   Wisconsin Residence, Eagle River, Wisconsin

1982   One South Wacker Office Building, Chicago, Illinois

1982   Addition to the Chicago Board of Trade, Chicago, Illinois

1983   Mercy Hospital Addition, Chicago, Illinois

1983   11 Diagonal Street, Johannesburg, South Africa

1984   University of Illinois Agricultural Engineering Science Building, Champaign, Illinois

1984   Learning Resources Center, College of Du Page, Glen Ellyn, Illinois

1984   Plaza East, Milwaukee, Wisconsin

1984   Shand Morahan Corporate Headquarters, Evanston, Illinois

1984   701 Fourth Avenue South, Minneapolis, Minnesota

1984   O'Hare Rapid Transit Station, Chicago, Illinois

1985   State of Illinois Center, Chicago, Illinois

1986   362 West Street, Durban, South Africa

1986   2 Energy Center, Naperville, Illinois

1986   Parktown Stands 85/879 and 102/103, Johannesburg, South Africa

BUILDINGS IN PROGRESS

North Western Terminal, Chicago, Illinois
Greyhound Terminal Project, Chicago, Illinois
O'Hare Airport Expansion Program, Chicago, Illinois
Park Avenue Tower, New York, New York
Southwest Center, Houston, Texas
Wilshire/Midvale Office Building, Los Angeles, California
Unifirst Center, Jackson, Mississippi
425 Lexington Avenue, New York, New York
City Center, New York, New York
Messe Frankfurt Convention Center, Frankfurt, West Germany
Hyatt Hotel, Frankfurt, West Germany
One Liberty Place, Philadelphia, Pennsylvania
North Loop Block #37, Chicago, Illinois
Von Aken Office Project, Shaker Heights, Ohio
Hyatt Amsterdam, Amsterdam, The Netherlands
Metro Mall, Chicago, Illinois

Houston Esplanade, Houston, Texas
Minnesota Convention Center, Minneapolis, Minnesota
120 N. La Salle Street, Chicago, Illinois
600 California Street, San Francisco, California
Naiman Company Sporting Clubs, Chicago, Illinois and Atlanta, Georgia
One Minneapolis Center, Minneapolis, Minnesota
750 Lexington Avenue, New York, New York
Second Avenue at 85th Street, New York, New York
Penn Yards, New York, New York
717 N. Michigan Avenue, Chicago, Illinois
Oakbrook Tower, Oakbrook, Illinois
Hawthorn Center Office Building, Vernon Hills, Illinois
Monarch Plaza, Atlanta, Georgia
South Ferry Terminal, New York, New York
Livingston Plaza, Brooklyn Heights, New York
Times Square, New York, New York
Fountain Square West, Cincinnati, Ohio

PROJECTS

1974 Georgia World Congress Center, Atlanta, Georgia
1974 World Forum, Atlanta, Georgia
1974 Rosemont Octagon, Rosemont, Illinois
1975 Hotel Ridgeway, Los Angeles, California
1976 State Office Building, Springfield, Illinois
1976 Conference City, Abu Dhabi, United Arab Emirates
1976 One Exchange Place, Chicago, Illinois
1976 Minnesota II, St. Paul, Minnesota
1978 Pahlavi National Library, Teheran, Iran
1978 North Loop Redevelopment, Chicago, Illinois
1979 First Chicago Metropolitan Operations Center, Elgin, Illinois
1980 St. Paul Convention Center, St. Paul, Minnesota
1981 Terminal de Transporte de Bogota, Bogota, Columbia
1982 Aspen House, Aspen, Colorado
1982 Humana Corporate Headquarters Competition, Louisville, Kentucky
1982 Codex Corporate Headquarters, Canton, Massachusetts
1982 Exposition and Office Complex, Chicago, Illinois
1982 Schaumburg Office Park, Schaumburg, Illinois
1984 San Diego Convention Center, San Diego, California
1985 North Loop Block #16, Chicago, Illinois
1985 10 Columbus Circle, New York, New York

AWARDS

Kemper Arena
1975   National AIA Honor Award
1975   Bartelt Award
1975   AIA Chicago Chapter Award
1975   AISC Award

Abu Dhabi Conference City
1976   Progressive Architecture Design
       Citation
1976   Prize in International Competition

Auraria Library
1976   AIA Chicago Chapter Award

Xerox Centre
1977   AIA Chapter Award
1977   Progressive Architecture Design
       Citation
1980   AIA Chicago Chapter Award

Michigan City Library
1977   AIA Chicago Chapter Award
1977   AIA Illinois Council Honor Award
1978   AIA American Library Association
       First Honor Award
1979   AISC Award

Minnesota II
1977   Winner in National Architecture
       Competition
1978   AIA Chicago Chapter Award
1978   Progressive Architecture Design
       Citation

St. Mary's Athletic Facility
1977   AIA Chicago Chapter Award
1977   AIA Illinois Council Honor Award
1978   AISC Award
1979   AIA National Honor Award

H. Roe Bartle Exhibition Hall
1978   AIA Chicago Chapter Award

La Lumiere Gymnasium
1968   AIA Chicago Chapter Award

Oak Brook Post Office
1978   AIA Chicago Chapter Award

**University of Illinois Agricultural
Engineering Science Building**
1978   AIA Chicago Chapter Award

Rust-Oleum Corporate Headquarters
1979   AIA Chicago Chapter Award
1979   Young Professional Award by
       *Building Design & Construction
       Magazine*
1979   AISC Award

Argonne Program Support Facility
1979   Owens-Corning Fiberglass Energy
       Conservation Award
1982   AIA Chicago Chapter Award

De La Garza Career Center
1981   ASHRAE Energy Award
1981   AIA Chicago Chapter Award

**Commonwealth Edison District
Headquarters**
1981   ASHRAE Energy Award

Addition to the Chicago Board of Trade
1982   Reliance Development Group,
       Inc., Second Annual Award for
       Distinguished Architecture
1983   AISC Award
1984   AIA Chicago Chapter Award
1985   Structural Engineering Association
       of Illinois

**Arnold W. Brunner Memorial Prize in
Architecture**
1982   Helmut Jahn

Area 2 Police Headquarters
1983   AIA Chicago Chapter Award

Chicago Central Area Plan
1985   Progressive Architecture Award

Plaza East Office Center
1985   Distinguished Architect Helmut
       Jahn
       City of Milwaukee Art Commission's
       1985 Annual Awards

State of Illinois Center
1985   Structural Engineering Association
       of Illinois
1986   AIA Chicago Chapter Award

ARCHITECTURAL VISITS

1966   Tour of United States
1971   Italy, Greece, Istanbul
1973/74 Paris, Germany
1975/76 London, Moscow, Paris, Abu
         Dhabi
1980   Spain, Morocco, Vienna, London,
         Copenhagen, Helsinki
1981   South Africa, Prague, Milan,
         Florence, Sienna, Venice, Verona
1982   South Africa, Nice, France
1982   London, Stockholm, Paris, South
         Africa
1983   South Africa, Sydney, Australia,
         Italy
1984   Frankfurt, Paris, South Africa,
         Zurich, Milan
1985   Frankfurt, Düsseldorf, Munich,
         Stuttgart, Hamburg, Berlin, Venice,
         Paris
1986   London, Paris, Tokyo

EXHIBITIONS

1974/84 Exhibitions, AIA Chicago Chapter Awards, The Art Institute of Chicago

1977 October Participant in symposium "State of the Art of Architecture/77," Graham Foundation, Chicago, Illinois

1977 Member, "Chicago 7"

1977 December Participant in group show "Exquisite Corpse," Walter Kelly Gallery, Chicago, Illinois

1978 December Participant in group show "Townhouses," Walker Art Center, Minneapolis, Minnesota

1979 Participant 25th Annual Progressive Architecture Awards Jury, New York, New York

1980 April Exhibition "City Segments," Walker Art Center, Minneapolis, Minnesota

1980 May Exhibition "Late Entries to the Chicago Tribune Competition," Museum of Contemporary Art, Chicago, Illinois

1980 June Exhibition "The Presence of the Past," representing the United States, Biennale, Venice, Italy; 1981–82 Paris, France; San Francisco, California

1980 August Exhibition "The Architectural Process," Young-Hoffman Gallery, Chicago, Illinois

1980 October Participant in symposium "Designing Today for Tomorrow," Architectural League of New York, New York, New York

1981 The Fort Worth Art Museum, Fort Worth, Texas

1981 January Exhibition "Chicago Architectural Drawing," Frumkin & Struve, Chicago, Illinois

1981 March Exhibition, The Chicago Architectural Club, Graham Foundation, Chicago, Illinois

1981 May Chicago International Art Exhibit, Navy Pier, Chicago, Illinois

1981 December Exhibition "Architecture as Synthesis," Harvard University, Graduate School of Design, Cambridge, Massachusetts

1981/82 May Arnold W. Brunner Memorial Prize, and exhibit, American Academy and Institute of Arts and Letters, New York, New York

1982 August Exhibition, The Chicago Architectural Club, The Art Institute of Chicago, Chicago, Illinois

1982 October Exhibition "Chicago Architects Design," The Art Institute of Chicago, Chicago, Illinois

1982 November Exhibition, Yale University School of Architecture, New Haven, Connecticut

1982 November Exhibition "Contemporary Chicago Architecture," Festival of the Arts, Northern Illinois University, DeKalb, Illinois

1983 February Exhibition "The Architect's Vision from Sketch to Final Drawing," The Chicago Historical Society, Chicago, Illinois

1983 February Exhibition "Current Projects," Thomas Beeby, Lawrence Booth, Helmut Jahn, Krueck and Olson, Stanley Tigerman, Young-Hoffman Gallery, Chicago, Illinois

1983 March Exhibition "Ornamentalism: The New Decorativeness in Architecture and Design," The Hudson River Museum, New York, New York; Archer M. Huntington Art Gallery, University of Texas, Austin, Texas

1983 May Exhibition "New Chicago Architecture 1983," The Art Institute of Chicago, Chicago, Illinois

1983 May Participant in symposium "Minneapolis Profile 1983," Walker Art Center, Minneapolis, Minnesota

1983 June Exhibition "Tall Buildings,"

The Southern Chapter Alberta Association of Architects, Calgary, Alberta, Canada

1983 September Exhibition "Design USA," Castello Sforzasco in the Sala Viscontea, Milan, Italy

1983 October Exhibition "Surface and Ornament," Puck Building, New York, New York

1983 October Exhibition "Competitions Won and Lost," San Francisco AIA Headquarters Gallery, San Francisco, California

1983 October Exhibition "150 Years of Chicago Architecture," Paris Art Center, Paris, France

1983 November Exhibition "1992 Chicago World's Fair Design Conference Drawings, New York, Los Angeles, Chicago," The University of Illinois, Chicago Campus, Chicago, Illinois

1983 November Exhibition "100 Years of Architectural Drawings in Chicago," Illinois Bell Telephone Company, Chicago, Illinois

1983 November Exhibition, The Chicago Architectural Club, "Tops" and Members' Work, The Art Institute of Chicago, Chicago, Illinois

1984 February Exhibition "Helmut Jahn," Ballenford Architectural Books and Gallery, Ltd., Toronto, Ontario, Canada

1984 March Exhibition "Chicago and New York, More Than a Century of Architectural Interaction," The Art Institute of Chicago, Chicago, Illinois; The A.I.A. Foundation, The Octagon, Washington, D.C.; Farish Gallery, Rice University, Houston, Texas; The New York Historical Society, New York, New York

1984 June Opening, permanent architectural collection, Deutsches Architekturmuseum, Frankfurt am Main, West Germany

1984 November Exhibition "Art and . . . . Architecture/Design." Moosart Gallery, Miami, Florida

1984 November Exhibition, The Chicago Architectural Club, Members' Work, The Art Institute of Chicago, Chicago, Illinois

1984 December Exhibition "The State of Illinois Center," University of Illinois, Champaign-Urbana, Illinois

1985 January Exhibition "Exhibition on Advanced Structures," Syracuse University, Syracuse, New York

1985 March Exhibition "Vu de l'Intérieur ou la Raison de l'Architecture" ("Looking from Inside or the Reason of Architecture"), Paris Biennale, Paris, France

1985 September/December Exhibition "Contemporary Landscape from the Horizon of Postmodern Design," The National Museums of Modern Art, Kyoto and Tokyo, Japan

1985 October Exhibition "150 Years of Chicago Architecture," Museum of Science and Industry, Chicago, Illinois

1986 January The Chicago Architectural Club, Betsy Rosenfield Gallery, Chicago, Illinois

1986 February Exhibition "Modernism Redux; Critical Alternatives," Grey Art Gallery and Study Center, New York University, New York, New York

1986 June Exhibition "Vision der Moderne," Deutsche Architectur Museum, Frankfurt, West Germany

1986 October "Helmut Jahn," Gallery MA, Tokyo, Japan

COLLABORATORS

JAMES GOETTSCH
Executive Vice President
Associate Director of Planning and Design

Projects, 1970 to date:
South Ferry Office Tower Proposal, New York, New York; Ten Columbus Circle Proposal, New York, New York; Broadway and 52nd Street Office Tower Competition, New York, New York; Penn Yards, New York, New York; 750 Lexington Avenue, New York, New York; Apt. Tower at 2nd Avenue, New York, New York; IBM/Park Tower, New York, New York; City Center, New York, New York; Two Energy Center, Naperville, Illinois; Parktown, Johannesburg, South Africa; 625 Michigan Avenue, Chicago, Illinois; 425 Lexington Avenue, New York, New York; 362 West Street, Durban, South Africa; Southwest Center, Houston, Texas; Park Avenue Tower, New York, New York; Chicago Transit Authority, Chicago, Illinois; Shand Morahan Corporate Headquarters, Evanston, Illinois; 11 Diagonal Street, Johannesburg, South Africa; State of Illinois Center, Chicago, Illinois; One South Wacker, Chicago, Illinois; DOE/ANL Program Support Facility, Argonne, Illinois; First National Bank at Xerox Centre, Chicago, Illinois; Xerox Centre, Chicago, Illinois; Glenbrook Professional Building, Glenview, Illinois; St. Mary's College Athletic Facility, Notre Dame, Indiana; Kemper Arena, Kansas City, Missouri.

SAM SCACCIA
Senior Vice President
Director of Production & Coordination

Projects, 1963 to date:
IBM/Park Tower, New York, New York; 750 Lexington Avenue, New York, New York; City Center, New York, New York; Parktown, Johannesburg, South Africa; 425 Lexington Avenue, New York, New York; Northwestern Atrium Center, Chicago, Illinois; Shand Morahan Corporate Headquarters, Evanston, Illinois; O'Hare Extension, Chicago, Illinois; 11 Diagonal Street, Johannesburg, South Africa; 362 West Street, Durban, South Africa; Park Avenue Tower, New York, New York; 701 Fourth Avenue South, Minneapolis, Minnesota; One South Wacker, Chicago, Illinois; Chicago Board of Trade Addition, Chicago, Illinois; Plaza East, Milwaukee, Wisconsin; First Source Center, South Bend, Indiana; College of Du Page Learning Resources Center, Glen Ellyn, Illinois; Agricultural Engineering Sciences Building, University of Illinois, Urbana, Illinois; DOE/ANL Program Support Facility, Argonne, Illinois; Cook County Jail Expansion, Chicago, Illinois; Area 2 Police Headquarters, Chicago, Illinois; Glenbrook Professional Building, Glenview, Illinois; Rust-Oleum Corporate Headquarters, Vernon Hills, Illinois; Williams Center Parking Facility 1 and 2, Tulsa, Oklahoma; Fourth

District Circuit Court Building, Maywood, Illinois; Hertz, Avis, National General Office and Maintenance Facilities, Chicago, Illinois; FAA Control Tower, Chicago-O'Hare, International Airport, Chicago, Illinois; American Airlines Concourse Expansion, United Airlines Tenant Alterations, Delta Airlines Concourse Additions, Trans World Airlines Concourse Additions, North Central Airlines Control Tower.

SCOTT PRATT
Vice President
Project Architect

Projects, 1971 to date:
One Hawthorne Place, Vernon Hills, Illinois; One Minneapolis Center, Minneapolis, Minnesota; Liberty Place, Philadelphia, Pennsylvania; Hyatt Hotel, Frankfurt, West Germany; Houston Esplanade, Houston, Texas; Minnesota Convention Center, Minneapolis, Minnesota; 600 California Street, San Francisco, California; Wilshire/Westwood, Los Angeles, California; Amax Headquarters Proposal, Indianapolis, Indiana; Dallas Arts District Project, Dallas, Texas; 701 South Fourth Avenue, Minneapolis, Minnesota; MIDCON Headquarters Proposal, Downers Grove, Illinois; Quorum/Woodfield Office Complex, Schaumburg, Illinois; CTA Clark/Lake Transfer Station, S.O.I.C., Chicago, Illinois; John Deere Harvester Works Office Facility, East Moline, Illinois; Deere & Company Iowa Computer Center, Davenport, Iowa; Mews on Larabee Townhouses, Chicago, Illinois; Sheffield Circle Townhouses, Chicago, Illinois; Agricultural Engineering Sciences Building, University of Illinois, Urbana, Illinois; Ohio-Fairbanks Project, Chicago, Illinois; Marriott Hotel, South Bend, Indiana; First Source Center, South Bend, Indiana; U.S. Post Office, Oak Brook, Illinois; W. W. Grainger Corporate Headquarters, Skokie, Illinois; Underground Parking Facility, Springfield, Illinois; State Office Building, Springfield, Illinois; Soldier Field Reconstruction Study, Chicago, Illinois; Arena Project, Rosemont, Illinois.

JAMES M. STEVENSON
Vice President
Project Architect

Projects, 1974 to date:
General Manager, O'Hare Associates (Joint Venture of Murphy/Jahn, Envirodyne Engineers and Schal Associates), Supervising Consultant for the O'Hare Development Program, Chicago, Illinois; O'Hare Rapid Transit Extension, O'Hare Terminal Station, System-wide Graphics, Fare Collection, Equipment and Escalators, Chicago, Illinois; Plaza East, Milwaukee, Wisconsin; Chicago-O'Hare International Airport: Comprehensive Signage System, Implementation of Phases I and II, Ticket Counter-Flight Information Study, Terminal Area Landscaping, Chicago, Illinois;

Chicago Central Area Transit Project, Chicago, Illinois; Four Horsemen Inn-Hotel Study, South Bend, Indiana; Area 2 Police Headquarters, Chicago, Illinois; Rust-Oleum Corporate Headquarters, Vernon Hills, Illinois; Cook County Jail Division One Modifications, Chicago, Illinois; La Lumiere Athletic Facility, La Porte, Indiana; Underground Parking Facility, Springfield, Illinois; CTA 87th Street Park and Ride, Chicago, Illinois; Richmond Courts Building, Richmond, Virginia; East Monroe Drive Underground Parking Facility, Chicago, Illinois.

RAINER SCHILDKNECHT
Vice President
Project Architect

Projects, 1978 to date:
Fountain Square West Project, Cincinnati, Ohio; Van Aken Project, Shaker Heights, Ohio; Hyatt Hotel, Frankfurt, Germany; Messe Frankfurt, Frankfurt, Germany; Unifirst Center Hotel & Office Building, Jackson, Mississippi; Northwestern Atrium Center, Chicago, Illinois; O'Hare People Mover System, Chicago, Illinois; O'Hare Maintenance Building, Chicago, Illinois; O'Hare Electrical Substation, Chicago, Illinois; Murphy/Jahn Office, Chicago, Illinois; Santa Fe Building Renovation, Chicago, Illinois; Greyhound Terminal, Chicago, Illinois; Chicago Board of Trade Addition, Chicago, Illinois; Plaza East, Milwaukee, Wisconsin; Area 2 Police Headquarters, Chicago, Illinois; Springfield Parking Structure and Hotel, Springfield, Illinois.

MARTIN FREDERICK WOLF
Vice President
Project Architect

Projects, 1978 to date:
Naiman Sports Club, Atlanta, Georgia; Penn Yards, New York, New York; United Airlines Terminal 1 Concourse B C, O'Hare International Airport, Chicago, Illinois; Manager of Architectural Design Services, O'Hare International Development Program, Chicago, Illinois; O'Hare International Airport Development Program, Chicago, Illinois; Southwest Center, Houston, Texas; Northwestern Atrium Center, Chicago, Illinois; Chicago Board of Trade Addition, Chicago, Illinois.

DENNIS RECEK
Vice President
Project Architect

Projects, 1968 to date:
Oakbrook Terrace Tower, Oakbrook, Illinois; Wilshire/Westwood, Los Angeles, California; Two Energy

Center, Naperville, Illinois; Shand Morahan Plaza, Evanston, Illinois; College of DuPage Learning Resources Center, Glen Ellyn, Illinois; Mercy Hospital Expansion, Chicago, Illinois; Electromotive Engineering Building, LaGrange, Illinois; Commonwealth Edison Bolingbrook District Headquarters, Bolingbrook, Illinois; Commonwealth Edison Transformer Substation No. 137, Chicago, Illinois; De La Garza Career Center, East Chicago, Indiana; La Lumiere School Gymnasium, LaPorte, Indiana; Michigan City Public Library, Michigan City, Indiana; Monroe Drive Underground Garage and Park Redevelopment, Chicago, Illinois.

NADA ANDRIC
Vice President
Director of Interior Design

Projects, 1971 to date:
IBM/Park Avenue, New York, New York; 625 North Michigan Avenue, Lobby Remodeling, Chicago, Illinois; Baker & McKenzie Global, Chicago, Illinois; Black Residence, New York, New York; United Airlines, Chicago, Illinois; Abelson-Taylor, Inc., Chicago, Illinois; Murphy/Jahn-Cupola, Chicago, Illinois; William A. Robinson, Inc., Chicago, Illinois; Murphy/Jahn Office, Chicago, Illinois; Northwestern Atrium Center, Chicago, Illinois; Southwest Center, Houston, Texas; Chicago Board of Trade Addition, Chicago, Illinois; State of Illinois Center, Chicago, Illinois; Latham & Watkins, Hedlund, Hunter & Lynch, Chicago, Illinois; AM International, Chicago, Illinois; First National Bank at Xerox Centre, Chicago, Illinois; Peat, Marwick, Mitchell & Co., Chicago, Illinois; Black Residence, Jackson, Wyoming; DOE/ANL Program Support Facility, Argonne, Illinois; Continental Bank Trust Department, Chicago, Illinois; The First National Bank of Chicago, Chairman of the Board Office Suite, Chicago, Illinois; Peat, Marwick, Mitchell & Co., Washington, D.C.; Seyfarth, Shaw, Fairweather & Geraldson, Chicago, Illinois; Walter E. Heller International, Chicago, Illinois; Lederer, Fox & Grove, Chicago, Illinois; Borg Warner, Chicago, Illinois; First Merchants National Bank, Michigan City, Indiana; The Canadian Consulate, Chicago, Illinois; Baker & McKenzie, Chicago, Illinois; Peat, Marwick, Mitchell & Co., Chicago, Illinois (1971); Brunswick Corporation, Skokie, Illinois; The First National Bank of Chicago, Plaza Level Auditorium, Chicago, Illinois.

PHILIP JOHN CASTILLO
Project Architect

Projects, 1978 to date:
Oakbrook Terrace Tower, Oakbrook, Illinois; Monarch Plaza II, Atlanta, Georgia; 717 N. Michigan Avenue Office Building, Chicago, Illinois; South Ferry Plaza Office Tower Proposal, New York, New York;

Ten Columbus Circle Proposal, New York, New York; Broadway and 52nd Street Office Tower Competition, New York, New York; North Loop Redevelopment: Block 16 and Block 37, Chicago, Illinois; Parktown Office Building, Johannesburg, South Africa; 362 West Street Office Building, Durban, South Africa; Southwest Center, Houston, Texas; Humana Corporate Headquarters Competition, Louisville, Kentucky; One South Wacker Office Building, Chicago, Illinois; IIT-Kent Law School, Chicago, Illinois; North Loop Transportation Center, Chicago, Illinois; Federal Life Insurance, Deerfield, Illinois.

MICHAEL PATTEN
Project Architect

Projects, 1984 to date:
City Center, New York, New York.

DANIEL DOLAN
Project Architect

Projects, 1979–1985:
Liberty Place, Philadelphia, Pennsylvania; Pacific Basin Tower, California; Houston Esplanade, Houston, Texas; 425 Lexington Avenue, New York, New York; Park Avenue Tower at 55th Street, New York, New York; Two Energy Center, Naperville, Illinois; 701 4th Avenue South, Minneapolis, Minnesota; Eagle River Residence, Eagle River, Wisconsin; Aspen Residence, Aspen, Colorado; Expo Park Exhibition/Office Complex, Chicago, Illinois; College of Du Page Learning Resources Center, Glen Ellyn, Illinois; Agricultural Engineering Sciences Building, University of Illinois, Urbana, Illinois.

DAVID HOVEY
Project Architect

Projects, 1974–1978:
Auraria Library, Denver, Colorado; La Lumiere Gymnasium, La Porte, Indiana; Rust-Oleum Corporate Headquarters, Vernon Hills, Illinois; De La Garza Career Center, East Chicago, Indiana.

WOJCIECH MADEYSKI
Project Architect

Projects, 1968–1976:
John Marshall Courts Building, Richmond, Virginia; Fourth District Courts Building, Maywood, Illinois.

WORKS REVIEWED IN BOOKS

Grube, Pran, Schultze, *100 Years of Architecture in Chicago,* Follet Co., 1976

Werner Blaser, *After Mies,* Van Nostrand Reinhold, 1977

Charles Jencks, *Late Modern Architecture,* Rizzoli International Publications, 1980

M. Lauber ed., *Beyond the Modern Movement,* Harvard Review, vol. 1, MIT Press, 1980

Muriel Emanuel ed., *Contemporary Architects,* St. Martin's Press, 1980

Werner Blaser, *Filigree Architecture,* Wepf & Co., 1980

Paul Goldberger, *The Skyscraper,* Alfred A. Knopf, 1981

Heinrich Klotz, *Jahrbuch für Architektur 1981/82,* Deutsches Architektur Museum, Friedr. Viewg. & Sohn, 1981

Werner Blaser, *Mies van der Rohe, Continuing the Chicago School of Architecture,* Birkhauser Verlag, 1981

Gerald Allen and Richard Oliver, *Architectural Drawing: The Art and The Process,* Whitney Library of Design, Watson-Guptill Publications, New York; The Architectural Press, London, 1981

Maurizio Casari and Vincenzo Pavan, eds., *New Chicago Architecture,* Rizzoli International Publications, 1981

The Chicago Architectural Club, *The Chicago Architectural Journal,* Rizzoli International Publications, 1981

Joseph J. Thorndike, Jr., ed., *Three Centuries of Notable American Architects,* American Heritage Publishing Co., New York, 1981

Chicago Architects Design, a Century of Architectural Drawings for the Art Institute of Chicago, The Art Institute of Chicago and Rizzoli International Publications, 1982

Peter Arnell and Ted Bickford, eds., *A Tower for Louisville, the Humana Competition,* Rizzoli International Publications, 1982

Werner Blaser, *Elemental Building Forms,* Beton-Verlag, 1982

The Chicago Architectural Club, *The Chicago Architectural Journal,* Rizzoli International Publications, vol. 2, 1982

Vittorio Magnago Lampugnani, *Architecture in Our Century in Drawings, Utopia and Reality,* Verlag Gerd Hatje, 1982

Heinrich Klotz, *Jahrbuch für Architektur 1983,* Deutsches Architektur Museum, Friedr. Viewg. & Sohn, 1983

Richard G. Saxon, *Atrium Buildings: Development and Design,* The Architectural Press, London, 1983

The Chicago Architectural Club, *The Chicago Architectural Journal,* Rizzoli International Publications, vol. 3, 1983

Peter Arnell and Ted Bickford, eds., *Southwest Center, the Houston Competition,* Rizzoli International Publications, 1983

Paolo Portoghesi, *Postmodern, the Architecture of the Postindustrial Society,* Rizzoli International Publications, 1984

Chicago and New York: Architectural Interactions, The Art Institute of Chicago, 1984

Heinrich Klotz, *Moderne und Postmoderne,* Friedr. Viewg. & Sohn, 1984

Heinrich Klotz, ed., *Die Revision der Moderne, Postmoderne Architektur 1960–1980,* Prestel, 1984

The Chicago Architectural Club, *The Chicago Architectural Journal,* Rizzoli International Publications, vol. 4, 1984

Alfredo de Vito, *Innovative Management Techniques: For Architectural Design and Construction,* Whitney Library of Design, Watson-Guptill Publications, New York, 1984

Ada Louise Huxtable, *The Tall Building Artistically Reconsidered: The Search for a Skyscraper Style,* Pantheon Books, New York, 1984

Christian K. Laine, ed., *The Chicago Architectural Annual 1985,* Metropolitan Press Publications, 1985

Pierre Mardaga, ed., *Biennale de Paris Architecture 1985*

A Style for the Year 2001, Shinkenchiku Co., Tokyo, 1985

Chris Johnson, ed., *The City in Conflict,* The Law Book Company Limited, North Ryde, NSW, Australia, 1985

Barbaralee Diamonstein, ed., *American Architecture Now II,* foreword by Paul Goldberger, Rizzoli International Publications, 1985

WORKS REVIEWED IN PERIODICALS

"Development of a Building System for Hospitals," *Bauen + Wohnen,* Zurich, March 1974

"Analysis of Planned and Completed Projects by C. F. Murphy Associates," *Bauen + Wohnen,* Zurich, September 1974

"Kemper Arena," *Architectural Record,* New York, March 1976

"Grand Structures," *Techniques + Architecture,* Paris, May 1976

"Kemper Arena," *Architectural Review,* London, June 1976

"Kemper Arena," *Inland Architect,* Chicago, June 1976

"Auraria Library," *Inland Architect,* Chicago, August 1976, November 1976

"Abu Dhabi Conference City," *Progressive Architecture,* New York, January 1977

"Minnesota II," *Engineering News Record,* New York, March 1977

"Kemper Arena," *Domus,* Milán, July 1977

"Auraria Library," *Domus,* Milan, July 1977

"Monroe Centre," *Inland Architect,* Chicago, October 1977

"CFMA Portfolio," *Architectural Review,* London, October 1977

"Auraria Library," *Architectural Record,* New York, November 1977

"Chicago's 1977 Awards," *Inland Architect,* Chicago, November 1977

"Michigan City Library," *Building Design and Construction,* Chicago, December 1977

"CFMA Portfolio," *L'Architectura,* Milan, December 1977

"Monroe Centre," *Progressive Architecture,* New York, January 1978

"Minnesota II," *Architecture Minnesota,* January/February 1978

"Chicago 7," *Inland Architect,* Chicago, February 1978

"CFMA Portfolio," *Domus,* Milan, April 1978

"Design Direction: Looking for What Is Missing," *AIA Journal,* Washington, May 1978

"Exquisite Corpse," "CFMA Portfolio," *A + U,* Tokyo, July 1978

"CFMA Portfolio," *Progressive Architecture,* New York, July 1978

"Pahlavi National Library," *Domus,* Milan, August 1978

"Chicago on the Drawing Boards," *Horizon,* September 1979

"Auraria Library," *A + U,* Tokyo, October 1978

"Minnesota II," *Progressive Architecture,* New York, January 1979

"St. Mary's Athletic Facility," *L'Industria delle Costruzioni,* Rome, February 1979

"Kansas City Convention Center," *Domus,* Milan, February 1979

"Kemper Arena/H. Roe Bartle," *AIA Journal,* Washington, March 1979

"Chicago Once," *Arquitectura,* Madrid, Spring 1979

"Argonne Program Support Facility," *Progressive Architecture,* New York, April 1979

"St. Mary's Athletic Facility," *Architectural Record,* New York, April 1979

"Kemper Arena," *Detail,* Germany, May/June 1979

"Athletic Facility in an Articulate Enclosure," *AIA Journal,* Washington, Mid-May 1979

"Abu Dhabi/UAE," *Domus,* Milan, June 1979

"New Designs and Directions at C. F. Murphy Associates," *Architectural Record,* New York, July 1979

"USA - Kansas City," *L'Industria delle Costruzioni,* Rome, July/August 1979

"St. Mary's College," *Detail,* Germany, July/August 1979

"The Time Is PM," *Chicago Magazine,* August 1979

"Corporate Headquarters Rises above Constraints of Small Site," *Building Design and Construction,* Chicago, September 1979

"Fourth District Courts Building"/"John Marshall Courts Building," *A + U,* Tokyo, September 1979

"Auraria Learning Center," *AIA Journal,* Washington, September 1979

"Chicago Architecture after Mies," *Critical Inquiry,* University of Chicago, Winter 1979

"Design Trends, Humanizing the Office Environment," *Real Estate Issues,* Winter 1979

"25th Annual PA Awards," *Progressive Architecture,* New York, January 1980

"La Lumiere Gymnasium," *Domus,* Milan, January 1980

"C. F. Murphy Associates, Five Projects," *GA Document,* 1, Tokyo, Spring 1980

"Glass Building Touted As Energy Showcase," *Building Design and Construction,* Chicago, April 1980

"Universitätssporthalle in Notre Dame," *Baumeister,* Germany, April 1980

"CFMA Office Building," *A + U,* Tokyo, April 1980

"The Building of the Year 2000," *Inland Architect,* Chicago, May 1980

"Glazed Structures," "Rust-Oleum Corporate Headquarters," *Domus,* Milan, May 1980

"Ein Franke in Chicago," *Der Architekt,* May 1980

"What's Next?" *AIA Journal,* Washington, Mid-May 1980

"Stadtische Bibliothek in Michigan City/USA," *Detail,* May/June 1980

"Recent Works of Chicago 7," *Architectural Review,* London, June 1980

"Chicago," *Progressive Architecture,* New York, June 1980

"Late Entries," *Progressive Architecture,* New York, June 1980

"The Tribune Competition 1922/1980," *Inland Architect,* Chicago, May 1980

"City Segments/Exhibition," *Inland Architect,* Chicago, June 1980

"Helmut Jahn Puts the State under Glass," *Chicago Magazine,* July 1980

"Chicago Story . . . " (Tribune Competition), *Horizon,* July 1980

"Three New Designs by C. F. Murphy Associates," *Architectural Record,* New York, August 1980

"Curves, Diagonals and Monochromatics," (First National Bank of Xerox Centre), *Inland Architect,* Chicago, July/August 1980

"H. Roe Bartle Exhibition Hall, Kansas City, Missouri," *Detail,* July/August 1980

"State of Illinois Center"/"Xerox Centre"/"Chicago Board of Trade Addition"/"One South Wacker"/"North Western Terminal," *GA Document,* 1, Tokyo, Spring 1980

"One South Wacker," *Inland Architect,* Chicago, September 1980

"Board of Trade Addition: A New Synthesis," *Inland Architect,* Chicago, September 1980

"Rust-Oleum Corporate Headquarters," *Baumeister,* Germany, September 1980

"Michigan City Library"/"St. Mary's Athletic Facility," *GA Document,* Tokyo, Special Issue, 1979–1980

"Illinois Center," *Architectural Review,* London, December 1980

"Xerox Centre," *Progressive Architecture,* New York, December 1980

"The Chicago Chapter/AIA 1980 Distinguished Building Awards," *Inland Architect,* Chicago, December 1980

"State of Illinois Center"/"Rust-Oleum Corporate Headquarters"/"St. Mary's Athletic Facility," *L'Architecture d'Aujourd'hui,* December 1980

"State of Illinois Center," *Progressive Architecture,* New York, February 1981

"11 Diagonal Street—South Africa's Most Futuristic Office Block," *Anglo-American Property Review,* vol. 4, no. 1, March 1981

"Xerox Centre," *GA Document,* 3, Tokyo, April 1981

"One South Wacker"/"Xerox Centre," *Architectural Review,* London, April 1981

"Xerox Centre"/"De La Garza Career Center"/"H. Roe Bartle Exhibition Hall"/"La Lumiere Gymnasium"/"High Rise Projects"/"Tribune Tower Late Entry"/"State of Illinois Center"/"First Bank Center"/"One South Wacker"/"Chicago Board of Trade Addition"/"Metropolitan Operations Center"/"Argonne National Laboratories"/"College of DuPage, Learning Resources Center"/"University of Illinois Agricultural and Engineering Sciences Building"/"U.S. Post Office"/"Private Residence," *Architecture and Urbanism,* Tokyo, April 1981

"Xerox Centre"/"Addition to the Chicago Board of Trade"/"North Western Terminal," *Domus,* Milan, April 1981

"Xerox Centre," *AIA Journal,* Washington, Mid-May 1981

"Helmut Jahn/Murphy Associates," *Controspazio,* April-August 1981

"Xerox Centre"/"De La Garza Career Center"/"Chicago Board of Trade Addition"/"One South Wacker"/"North Western Terminal"/"State of Illinois Center"/"High Rise Projects," *Bauen + Wohnen,* Zurich, June 1981

"A Lively Neocon—Thonet Takes Five," *Progressive Architecture,* New York, August 1981

"State of Illinois Center"/"Xerox Centre"/"One South Wacker"/"Chicago Board of Trade"/"North Western Terminal," *Techniques + Architecture,* Paris, September 8, 1981

"Jahn's Designs Shatter the Box," *Engineering News Record,* October 8, 1981

"The Changing Skins of Helmut Jahn," *AIA Journal,* Washington, October 1981

"Thonet Takes 5, Take Thonet," *Interior Design,* October 1981

"Steel 25 Congress," *Architecture SA,* October 1981

"Master Builders of the Windy City," *Life,* November 1981

"How Helmut Jahn Is Changing the Face of Chicago," *Crain's Chicago Business,* November 9, 1981

"Three Designs by Murphy/Jahn,"/"North Western Terminal Project"/"Railway Exchange Building Renovation"/"O'Hare Rapid Transit Station," *Architectural Record,* New York, December 1981

"Helmut Jahn on Architecture as Synthesis," Harvard Graduate School of Design, *News,* Winter 1982

"Interiors' Awards—Four on the Jury," *Interiors,* January 1982

"Niedlasslung eines E-Werkes in Bolingbrook," "Commonwealth Edison District Headquarters," *Baumeister,* Germany, February 1982

"Chicago's Building Boom: Architecture Is Up to Date in the Windy City," Peat, Marwick, Mitchell & Co., *World,* no. 1, 1982

"Someplace to Be Somebody," *Chicago Magazine,* April 1982

"Chicago: La Griglia, L'Infinito," "Addition to the Chicago Board of Trade," *Domus,* Milan, March 1982

"Helmut Jahn's Indiana Buildings," *Tribune* (South Bend, Ind)., Michiana Section, Sunday, May 16, 1982

"State of the Arts—Architecture—The New Chicago," *American Arts,* May 1982

"Les Nouveaux Gratte-Ciel Américains—La Cinquième Génération," "One South Wacker"/"Addition to the Board of Trade"/"North Western Terminal"/"Xerox Centre," *L'Architecture d'Aujourd'hui,* April 1982

"Teutonisches Wunderkind," *Der Spiegel,* no. 27, July 5, 1982

"Helmut Jahn Topples the Box," "Addition to the Chicago Board of Trade"/"North Western Terminal"/"No. 11 Diagonal Street"/"St. Mary's Athletic Facility"/"Kemper Arena"/"Xerox Centre"/"State of Illinois Center," *Architect & Builder,* Johannesburg, June 1982

"Architecture as a Corporate Asset," "Addition to the Chicago Board of Trade," *Business Week,* October 4, 1982

"Energy Savings in the Round," "Argonne Program Support Facility," *Building Design and Construction,* Chicago, October 1982

"Tall Tower for Texas," "Bank of the Southwest Tower"/"Addition to the Chicago Board of Trade"/"Xerox Centre," *Time,* November 8, 1982

"The Sky's the Limit," "Bank of the Southwest Tower"/"Xerox Centre"/"State of Illinois Center"/"North Western Terminal," *Newsweek,* November 8, 1982

"A New Era Dawns for First Source," "First Source Center," *Corporate Design,* November-December 1982

"Chicago," "Xerox Centre"/"State of Illinois Center"/"North Western Terminal," *Holland Herald,* vol. 17, no. 12, 1982

"State of Illinois Center"/"One South Wacker"/"Xerox Centre"/"Bank of the Southwest Tower," *Europeo,* no. 52, December 27, 1982

"Architecture on the Rise," "Bank of the Southwest Tower," *Harper's Bazaar,* January 1983

"Best of Chicago—Best New Skyscraper," "One South Wacker," *Chicago Magazine,* January 1983

"Toward Romantic Hi Tech," "Area 2 Police Headquarters"/"Argonne Program Support Facility"/"First Source Center," *Architectural Record,* New York, January 1983

"State of Illinois Center"/"Argonne Program Support Facility," *SD—Space Design,* February 1983

"Murphy/Jahn," First Source Center"/"Argonne National Laboratories Chicago Branch—Department of Energy"/"Area 2 Police Center"/"United States Post Office," *A + U,* Tokyo, February 1983

"North Western Terminal," *Bunte,* no. 6, March 2, 1983

"Glass Highlights Design of Bank/Hotel Complex,

First Source Center," *Building Design and Construction,* Chicago, March 1983

"Jahn's Chicago 1. Board of Trade," "Jahn's Chicago 2. One South Wacker," "The Sixth Annual Review of New American Architecture," *AIA Journal,* Washington, May 1983

"Chicago Design: In Search of a New Order," "Murphy/Jahn Interiors," *Interiors,* May 1983

"New Chicago Architecture," "Bank of the Southwest Tower," *Inland Architect,* Chicago, May/June 1983

"362 West St.—Romantic Hi-Tech—An Interview with Helmut Jahn," "362 West St."/"11 Diagonal St.," *Planning 61 and Building Developments,* Saxonwold, South Africa, March/April 1983

"Today's Towers: Reaching for New Heights," "Bank of the Southwest Tower"/"Humana Corporation Competition," *American Arts,* May 1983

"Murphy/Jahn," "Bank of the Southwest Tower"/"Addition to the Chicago Board of Trade," *World Construction and Engineering,* vol. 2, no. 10, Tokyo, June 1983

"Architects' Notebooks," "We're on Our Way to O'Hare," *Inland Architect,* Chicago, July/August 1983

"Murphy/Jahn," "North Western Terminal"/"Greyhound Terminal," *World Construction and Engineering,* vol. 2, no. 11, Tokyo, July 1983

"Murphy/Jahn," "11 Diagonal St."/"One South Wacker," *World Construction and Engineering,* vol. 2, no. 12, Tokyo, August 1983

"The Neocon Winners," "Surface and Ornament ColorCore Competition—Helmut Jahn Invitational Entry," *Interiors,* August 1983

"High-Tech: Britain v. America," "Argonne Program Support Facility"/"First Source Center," *Architectural Review,* London, August 1983

"Murphy/Jahn—Recent Works and Projects," "State of Illinois Center"/"Oak Brook Post Office"/"First Source Center"/"Argonne Program Support Facility"/"Addition to the Chicago Board of Trade"/"One South Wacker"/"Bank of the Southwest Tower"/"11 Diagonal Street"/"701 Fourth Avenue South"/"Greyhound Terminal"/"362 West Street"/"Americana Plaza"/"Shand Morahan Plaza"/"Wilshire/Midvale"/"North Loop Block F," *GA Document,* 7, Tokyo, September 1983

"The House That Big Jim Built," "State of Illinois Center," *Chicago Magazine,* September 1983

"Helmut Jahn," "One South Wacker"/"North Western Terminal," *Gentlemen's Quarterly,* September 1983

"Architecture: Chicago's Skyscraping Romantic—Helmut Jahn," "North Western Terminal"/"Bank of the Southwest Tower," *Interview,* September 1983

"Eight Experts Review City's New Skyline," "State of Illinois Center"/"One South Wacker," *Crain's Chicago Business,* August 1, 1983

"Round Peg State Center Fits into City of Square Holes," "State of Illinois Center," *Engineering News Record,* September 22, 1983

"An Insider's Guide to Chicago," *Travel and Leisure,* September 1983

"A Bold New Breed of Buildings Is Reaching Towards the Skies," "One South Wacker"/"Xerox Centre"/"Bank of the Southwest Tower," *Smithsonian,* October 1983

"Helmut Jahn (Murphy/Jahn)," "Addition to the Chicago Board of Trade"/"One South Wacker"/"State of Illinois Center"/"701 Avenue South"/"362 West Street"/"Bank of the Southwest Tower"/"11 Diagonal Street"/"MGIC Plaza East"/"John Deere Harvester Works Office"/"Shand Morahan Office Building"/"Greyhound Terminal"/"Chicago-O'Hare International Airport Development Program"/"North Western Terminal"/"Wilshire/Midvale," *A + U,* Tokyo, November 1983

"Helmut Jahn," "One South Wacker"/"Addition to the Chicago Board of Trade"/"Bank of the Southwest Tower"/"11 Diagonal Street"/"First Source Center," *Vogue Living,* Sidney, November 1983

"Genesis of a Tower: Helmut Jahn Drawings," "Bank of the Southwest Tower," *AIA Technology,* Fall 1983

"Skyscrapers and the City," "State of Illinois Center"/"Bank of the Southwest Tower," *Chicago History,* Winter 1983–84

"Helmut Jahn Four Towers, 1978–82," "Addition to the Chicago Board of Trade"/"One South Wacker"/"Humana"/"Bank of the Southwest Tower," *Architectural Review,* 7/8, London, 1983

"Can Chicago Architecture Live Up to Its Past?," "One South Wacker"/"State of Illinois Center"/"Addition to the Chicago Board of Trade"/"Xerox Centre"/"North Western Terminal," *The New Art Examiner,* January 1984

"Architecture: Helmut Jahn," "Robert L. Murphy, Eagle River, Wisconsin House," *Architectural Digest,* March 1984

"Residence—Eagle River, Wisconsin, U.S.A., Murphy/Jahn," *L'Architecture d'Aujourd'hui,* April 1984

"One South Wacker," *L'Industria delle Costruzioni,* Rome, July 1984

"Jeu d'Enveloppes"/"Un Rond dans L'eau," "First Source Center"/"Argonne Program Support Facilities," *Techniques + Architecture,* Paris, September 1984

"Chicago Skyscrapers: Romanticism and Reintegration," "Addition to the Chicago Board of Trade," *Domus,* Milan, September 1984

"Helmut Jahn's Latest Glass-Clad Building in Chicago," "One South Wacker," *Architect & Builder,* Johannesburg, November 1984

"Prominent Persons in High Tech Architecture—Helmut Jahn," "Parktown, 1983–86"/"Chicago O'Hare International Airport Development Program 1982–89"/"362 West Street 1982–1985," *SD—Space Design,* January 1985

"Chicago Now," "State of Illinois Center"/"Murphy/Jahn"/"North Western Terminal"/"Xerox Centre"/"One South Wacker"/"State of Illinois Center"/"Chicago Board of Trade"/"O'Hare Rapid Transit Station," *Nikkei Architecture,* January 28, 1985

"Refining the Manhattan Skyline: Three New Projects by Murphy/Jahn," "City Center"/"Park Avenue Tower"/"425 Lexington Avenue"; "William J. Le Messurier's Super-Tall Structures: A Search for the Ideal," "Bank of the Southwest Tower," *Architectural Record,* New York, January 1985

"The Xerox Centre High-Rise in Chicago, Illinois," "Xerox Centre," *L'Industria Italiana del Cemento,* January 1985

"Private Residence, Eagle River, Wisconsin," *GA Houses,* 17, Tokyo, January 1985

"Private Developer Seeks Innovative Designer," "425 Lexington," *Urban Design International,* Winter 1985

"The Battle of Starship Chicago," "State of Illinois Center," *Time,* February 4, 1985

"High-Rise, Hard Sell," "425 Lexington"/"Park Avenue Tower," *New York Magazine,* March 11, 1985

"Chicago: Big, Bad and Beautiful," "State of Illinois Center," *M: The Civilized Man,* May 1985

"High-Tech Expansion: Chicago-O'Hare International Airport Development Program," *Architectural Record,* New York, May 1985

"Inside Helmut Jahn's State of Illinois Triumph—A Search for Excellence," "State of Illinois Center"/"CTA Station—O'Hare"/"United Airlines Terminal"/"Murphy/Jahn Cupola"/"Plaza East Office Center"/"425 Lexington"/"City Center"/"Park Avenue Tower"; "The Master Builder," "State of Illinois Center"/"Xerox Centre"/"One South Wacker," *Gentlemen's Quarterly,* May 1985

"Chicago's Ancient Monuments: The State of Illinois Center with Three Illustrations by the Author," "Two Additions: The Chicago Board of Trade and Northwestern's Law School," *Inland Architect,* Chicago, May/June 1985

"Der Schnellste Colt Imganzen Westen: Jahn-Bau State of Illinois Center in Chicago," "State of Illinois Center," *Der Spiegel,* no. 24, June 10, 1985

"City Limits," "State of Illinois Center," *AJ,* no. 24, vol. 181, London, June 12, 1985

"Residence in Eagle River," *A + U,* Tokyo, July 1985

"Philadelphia's Sacred Cap Finally Falls Victim to a Developer's Lofty Ambitions," *Architectural Record,* New York, July 1985

"The O'Hare Station—Last Link to the Loop," *Inland Architect,* Chicago, July/August 1985

"Works of Murphy/Jahn," "11 Diagonal Street"/"701 Fourth Avenue South"/"Plaza East"/"College of DuPage"/"Shand Morahan Office Headquarters"/"O'Hare Rapid Transit"/"University of Illinois Agricultural/Engineering Science Building," *A + U,* Tokyo, October 1985

"Ein Mann Baut Bunt" ("A Man Builds Bountifully"), "Southwest Center"/"State of Illinois Center"/"One South Wacker"/"Shand Morahan Plaza"/"O'Hare Rapid Transit Station"/"Oakbrook Post Office"/"Penn Yards," *Stern Magazin,* 40, September 26, 1985

"State of Illinois Center," *GA Document,* 13, Tokyo, November 1985

PHOTOGRAPH CREDITS

All photographs are by Keith Palmer and James R. Steinkamp jointly, except as noted below.

Doug Hill p. 218

Timothy Hursley © The Arkansas Office pp. 84 (right), 94 (top), 116

Helmut Jahn pp. 32, 33, 34, 35, 194, 226

Paul Kivett pp. 20, 21, 22, 23, 24, 25, 26, 27, 28, 29

Nathaniel Lieberman pp. 208 (top left), 209, 234, 237

Barbara Elliot Martin p. 30

Michael Meyersfeld pp. 151, 152, 153

Keith Palmer pp. 38, 47, 48, 49, 50, 52, 74, 75, 240

Skyline Studio pp. 189, 193, 194, 195

James R. Steinkamp pp. 43, 54, 70, 85, 88, 93, 94 (left and bottom), 95, 99, 102, 112, 113, 117, 118, 119, 120, 121, 122, 123, 127, 129, 130, 131, 133, 146, 147, 148, 149, 165, 166, 168, 172, 176, 183, 187, 197, 207, 226, 227, 228, 235, 242, 243, 245, 250, 251

RENDERINGS AND DRAWINGS

Manuel Auila (assistant) p. 229

Michael Budilovsky pp. 162 (bottom, middle, and right), 166, 213, 222, 232, 233, 244, 246, 249 (assistant): pp. 109, 111 (top left), 156, 167, 181, 186, 208 (right), 214 (left), 223, 231, 238, 243, 250, 251, 252

Bob Crone (assistant) p. 181 (left)

Dan Dolan pp. 84, 105, 131, 138, 139, 241

James Goetsch p. 167

John Leahy (assistant) p. 159

Pat Lopez pp. 185, 207, 208 (bottom), 210, 214 (right), 215

Slutsky and Associates p. 236

Jim Smith pp. 163, 165, 184, 206, 216, 230, 248

Kevin Woest pp. 136, 155, 161, 162 (bottom left), (assistant): p. 63

Martin Wolf p. 111 (bottom left, middle, and bottom right)

Woods p. 219

PRESENT EMPLOYEES

Meg Abraham, Lou Aiello, Enrique Anaya, Nada Andric, Alma Aquino, Ed Antonio, Marybeth Armstrong, Tisha Bauer, Gordon Beckman, Rita Berget, Randy Bremhorst, Mike Bretz, Mike Budilovsky, Earl Burris, Arlan Cable, Phil Castillo, Michael Chalmers, Tom Chambers, Andrew Cohen, Loretta Cohen, Steve Cook, Katalin Demeter, Maritza Demski, Ted Depaz, Dan Dorcy, Jim Economos, Nancy Eggen, Ed Ehlert, Tom Fabian, Brian Favia, Mark Frisch, Susan Froelich, Steve Fuller, Maggie Furjanic, Jose Gelats, Geri Glineke, Hilmer Goedeking, James Goettsch, Robert Goldberg, Sandy Gorshow, Virginia Greene, Kevin Havens, Bruce Haxton, Peter Hayes, Louis Hedgecock, Robert Hendrickson, Art Herbstman, Lori Hladek, Robert Hogan, Ruben Jaurigue, Horst Jentschura, Mark Jolicoeur, Hovie Jones, Joan Kaiser, Mike Kaiserauer, David Karlquist, Steve Kern, Dale Kidd, MaryJo Koldenhoven, Fred Koziol, Evelyn Kroczek, Ray Krupa, Anne Kubicki, Alison Kukla, Thomas Kulpa, Steven Lambrin, John Landry, Steve Larson, Rick Levin, Kai Lie, Richard Linblade, Vern Lohman, Bill Lohmann, Kathleen Machek, Larry Madigan, Christopher Manfre, Hector Marquez, Martiano Martinez, Frank Massey, Kent Meihofer, Sara Mills, Anthony Mosellie, Charles Murphy, Douglas Muska, John Myefski, Kathy Nelligan, Donna Nelson, Holger Nettbaum, Steven Nilles, Steve Nitekman, Lori North, Brian O'Connor, James O'Malley, Michael Orr, Keith Palmer, Mike Patten, Rad Pejovic, Tony Pelipada, Mark Piltingsrud, Andy Piraro, Jon Pohl, John Pohling, Scott Pratt, Pat Pruchnik, Steve Pynes, Lou Raia, Dennis Recek, Greg Recht, John Ronning, Michele Rudolph, Sam Scaccia, Rainer Schildknecht, Sudheir Shinde, Wojciech Sienczyk, Sudarshan Soni, Scott Sonic, Gregory Soyka, Sherry Spaulding, Lori Splinter, Jim Steinkamp, Charlie Stetson, James Stevenson, Charlie Sullivan, Scott Thomas, Ed Urbanczyk, Allen Villanueva, Ed Wilkas, Eberhard Wimmer, Richard Winokur, Susan Winstead, Martin Wolf, Mike Yasine